A Kids' Power Book

Shannen and the Dream for a School

JANET WILSON

Second Story Press

Library and Archives Canada Cataloguing in Publication

Wilson, Janet, 1952-
Shannen and the dream for a school / by Janet Wilson.

(The kids' power series)
ISBN 978-1-926920-30-6

1. Koostachin, Shannen, 1994-2010. 2. Indian activists—
Ontario—Attawapiskat—Biography. 3. Children's rights—
Ontario—Attawapiskat—Juvenile literature. 4. Cree children—
Education—Ontario—Attawapiskat—Juvenile literature.
I. Title. II. Series: Kids' power series

E90.K66W55 2011   j971.004'97323092   C2011-904497-8

Third Printing 2012

Edited by Yasemin Ucar
Designed by Melissa Kaita
Icons © iStockphoto

Printed and bound in Canada

*Second Story Press gratefully acknowledges the support of the
Ontario Arts Council and the Canada Council for the Arts for our
publishing program. We acknowledge the financial support of the
Government of Canada through the Canada Book Fund.*

ONTARIO ARTS COUNCIL
CONSEIL DES ARTS DE L'ONTARIO

Canada Council   Conseil des Arts
for the Arts   du Canada

MIX
Paper from
responsible sources
FSC
www.fsc.org   FSC® C004071

Published by
SECOND STORY PRESS
20 Maud Street, Suite 401
Toronto, ON M5V 2M5
www.secondstorypress.ca

Contents

"When I shook his hand, I told him that we're not going to quit."

Shannen Koostachin, *The Globe and Mail*
Quote of the Day, May 30, 2008

Author's Note

"When you know other children have big comfy schools with hallways that are warm, you feel like you don't count for anything."

Shannen Koostachin, 13, Attawapiskat First Nation, Ontario, Canada

Shannen had a dream—that all First Nations children be educated in decent schools, the kind non-Native children attend. The story you are about to read is the true story of Shannen and her classmates' efforts to get the Canadian government to replace their contaminated elementary school in Attawapiskat First Nation, in northern Ontario.

To get to Attawapiskat, imagine traveling north by car or train until the roads and rails end. From there, you'd have to take a small airplane even farther north over the flat, vast muskeg until you reach the western shore of James Bay. The reserve of two thousand or so people is at the mouth of the Attawapiskat River.

The events in this story really happened and the characters are real, however, my telling of the story has been fictionalized. I have imagined most of the dialogue, inspired by the recollections of many of the people involved and, with their blessing, have taken small artistic liberties in recreating some of the situations. Newspaper articles, speeches, and quotes from government officials, are accurate, but at times abbreviated.

Attawapiskat, seen here from an airplane,
is home to about 2,000 people.

March 9, 2009, Attawapiskat First Nation, Ontario, Canada

Winter mornings in Attawapiskat are normally quiet—so quiet that most days the loudest sound other than the occasional bark of a dog or the *braaap* of a snowmobile engine is the squeak, squeak of children's boots making their way along the snow-packed road. This was not one of those mornings.

The first bangs and crashes that echoed through the reserve pulled children like a magnet from every direction toward the source—the old J.R. Nakogee Elementary School. Yellow bulldozers, dump trucks, and praying mantis-like excavators had driven up the winter ice road along the James Bay coast to take their positions in the schoolyard. In the morning, the children pressed moose-hide mittens against the chain-link fence and peered through cracks in the black plastic tarpaulin. Older kids scrabbled up snow banks to get a better look at the demolition site—until finally the children were shooed away to their classes in the nearby portables.

Schoolchildren had walked past the ghostly gray building every morning and every afternoon for so long they barely noticed it. Most didn't remember the day, nine years before, when angry and frustrated parents nailed boards over the windows and doors, and refused to allow their children to enter the building. Since then, the only children who had been inside were those daring enough to lower themselves through a hole in the roof to play in the rooms some say were haunted with the spirits of departed children.

This was a sad day for those residents of Attawapiskat who remembered when J.R. Nakogee School first opened in 1976. Children had been excited to attend school in the bright and clean building that had electricity and indoor plumbing—luxuries only a few Attawapiskat households enjoyed at that time. Parents had been happy that their children would now stay in the community to be educated instead of being sent far away to school in the south. The school became the heart of the community, where everyone had come together for Powwows, Feasts, socials, square dances, monster bingos, and other special events. The people of Attawapiskat had been proud of their new school.

The problems began with the dreadful discovery that the underground iron pipe carrying diesel fuel to the school's furnace had leaked tens of thousands of litres into the soil. For years, teachers and parents complained that their children were tired, sick, and irritable. Even though health reports on the spill indicated that dangerous chemicals had been detected, the Canadian government, which was responsible for maintenance, declared that there were no health concerns in the school. Finally, the parents said, "Enough is enough!" and the building was boarded up, and had remained closed ever since.

On this day, nine years later, the children sitting in nearby portables were finding it hard to concentrate with all the noise of the demolition. Unlike their parents, many of the students were not feeling sad. To them, the old school was just a haunting reminder of what a real school was like—with a library, a gym, and halls, all under the same roof. Once the building was finally gone, maybe they would get a new school. Maybe they wouldn't have to ask each other, "If children in other communities have decent schools, why don't we?"

TOP: J.R. Nakogee School
BOTTOM: The demolition of J.R. Nakogee School

CHAPTER 1
The Forgotten Children

"Education is important because in the future you'll have a better life. Because without an education, you wouldn't have a job or go anywhere at all."

Shannen Koostachin, 13, Attawapiskat, 2008

"Shut the door!" a chorus of voices hollered as Shannen blew into the portable on an icy blast of James Bay wind. She pushed hard on the door three times before it closed, stomped the snow from her boots, and headed straight to her desk. Her coat and mittens were staying on for now.

"Holay cow, it's like a freezer in here," cried Shannen, shivering. "My toes are Popsicles." Shannen clasped her hands together as in prayer. "Pleeeeeease can I leave my boots on, Carinna?" she pleaded. "My toes will snap if I pull off my boots."

The new, young teacher knew the rules—no boots in class. She sat cross-legged behind her desk, her own feet tucked under her legs for warmth. She held up two fingers in a peace sign—her code for "Okay." Shannen flashed her teacher a wide smile and blew into her mittens.

"I can't write in class today, Carinna," Chris called out. "My fingers are frozen stiff!"

None of the other dozen or so kids in the small portable laughed at his joke. Shannen was not surprised. Her friends were usually grumpy after the sub-Arctic winter walks to school.

"I should have stayed in bed," Shannen whimpered. She shivered as she pulled off her hat. When she shook out her blue-black hair, it draped her dark eyes like a curtain.

Emma sniffed, "Ha! *Ki-kinaskin,* ShanShann. You wouldn't miss school even if you had the chance."

Shannen gave Emma her signature eyes-wide-open glare—even though it was true, Shannen really did like school. She almost always felt eager to get to class, once she managed to drag herself out of bed. She especially enjoyed hanging out with her friends. Growing up together in this tightly knit community, they were really more like family. They even called each other brother and sister.

It wasn't that she liked the work—she would rather do anything than homework—but Shannen knew that education was important. Her parents were always reminding her and her brothers and sisters, "Education is the key that unlocks the door to a brighter future." Shannen often wondered what that brighter future might be. She changed her life plans as often as her hairstyle. One day she wanted to work in a school like her mother, the next, for the band council like her father. Lately, Shannen had the same dream as her older sister—to be a model. However, she had some growing to do if she was going to be anywhere near as tall as Serena.

And even though she wasn't a big fan of working, Shannen did enjoy the learning that came with it. Her favorite subject was Cree, because she liked learning about her language and culture. Elders showed them how to make dreamcatchers, moccasins from caribou and moose hide, and sew tiny beads in Cree patterns. Shannen enjoyed learning to dance and sing to perform at Powwows. She felt comforted by the familiar smoky scent of sweetgrass, cedar, and sage burning at smudges, sweatlodges, and other traditional ceremonies. Not all the kids in Attawapiskat felt the same way.

Shannen worried about her friends who talked about quitting school. Kids who left school were more likely to be bored and get into trouble. Some of the girls wanted to get married and have babies, but Shannen was planning to graduate from university and experience life off the reserve for a while before she came back home to start a family.

More frigid wind blasted in with Jonah. "Shut the door!"

"We'd be warm and cozy if we had a real school instead of a bunch of leaky old portables," complained Shannen, slumping miserably into the back of the chair. A real school had halls, an art room, computer labs, a cafeteria, and a library all in the same building. "I can't wait to go to Vezina next year," she added. Serena was already at Vezina High School but she was not nearly as enthusiastic. Last year there was talk of Serena going off the reserve to a school in the south for a better education, but in the end, she couldn't bear the thought of leaving her family. Shannen totally understood. Apart from anything else, it would break their great-grandmother's heart. *Jaban* didn't think children should have to leave their home and their loved ones for a good education.

"How much longer do we have to wait before they build the new school, Shannen?" asked Ashley.

Ashley and Shannen in class, with Nelleon Scott in the background

"Don't ask me," Shannen said, already regretting that she had opened this can of worms.

Chris chimed in. "Walking from portable to portable sucks. As soon as we get warmed up, we have to go back into the freezing cold."

"It's too late for us, anyway," said Ashley. "But at least our kid brothers and sisters will go to a real school."

"Yeah, at least they'll have a gym inside, instead of having to walk ten minutes to the sports arena," added Solomon.

"Remember when the guidance counselor saw us come out of gym class all warm and sweaty?" Stephanie asked, starting to giggle. "It was 40 below and he said that all he could see was fog above our heads!"

"What's so funny about that?" Chris was scowling. "I get headaches from the cold."

"And they won't have mice eating their snacks," Jonah said with a shudder.

Shannen grimaced. "And they won't have their washroom so close to their class. It's embarrassing."

Solomon added, "It's even more embarrassing when the pipes freeze!"

"I like when the pipes freeze." Brendon chuckled. "Then we get to go home."

"Maybe the government is frozen," Chris said, angrily. "They promised almost three years ago to build a school but we're still waiting in crappy portables."

"Ha! If you think we're ever going to get a new school, you're dreaming," Jonah scoffed, yanking the peak of Chris's cap. "Get real! The government doesn't care about us. We're just a bunch of Indians living in the middle of nowhere, far away from their rich buildings in Ottawa."

Shannen winced. Jonah was saying what most people on the reserve actually felt. Their leaders were always dealing with the government over one problem or another—bad water, over-crowded housing, poverty, and of course, the new school.

Her *mooshoom* (grandfather) had been working on plans for the school since the old building was condemned. And three years ago, Serena had traveled to the capital of Canada to tell

Janet Kioke at her desk in the grade eight portable with Stephanie Paulmartin and Brendon Kioke in the background.

the government that the students of J.R. Nakogee School were tired of waiting. "I think that we are the forgotten children of Ontario," she said to the Indian Affairs minister. He shook her hand and promised a new school. All across the country, newspapers printed Serena's quotes about children on reserves being treated like second-class citizens. Serena was a hero in Attawapiskat. But not everyone trusted the government.

Shannen said, "These things take time, Jonah. The minister promised."

Jonah threw his head back and laughed. "So what! You can't trust what white people say."

Chris and Solomon nodded.

"But Jonah, lots of white kids wanted us to get a school, too," Shannen said. Children off the reserve had written letters to

The grade eight portable was cold and drafty in winter.

the government ministers, asking them to keep their promise. They called their campaign Students-Helping-Students. "And a promise is a promise," Shannen added. Shannen knew that promises were sacred. If she was not allowed to break a promise, the government should not be allowed to, either.

Jonah sneered. "Oh yeah, like the government would never break a promise to Indians. Shannen, wake up! We're not getting a new school."

Snickers rippled through the room. Shannen could feel her cheeks burn. I'll ask Serena when the construction will begin, she said to herself. I'll prove to Jonah that he doesn't know what he's talking about.

Carinna stood up and tried to get her students' attention. Brendon put his hand over his mouth and made a piercing *a'honk-a'honk* that made the teacher jump. All the kids laughed.

Carinna frowned but Shannen was grateful for the interruption.

"Please remind your parents that tomorrow there's another planning meeting for the grad trip," Carinna announced.

It was an Attawapiskat tradition that grade eight students celebrate their graduation with a trip south. The students this year were hotly debating two destinations—Niagara Falls and Canada's Wonderland. The Falls might be one of the Seven Natural Wonders of the World, but none of the kids was denying that the real draws were the unnatural wonders of video games and shopping malls. Shannen was pushing for Canada's Wonderland. It had the most thrilling rides and biggest roller coasters in North America, and it was just north of Toronto, a big city thousands of times more exciting than Attawapiskat.

"There will be another bake sale fundraiser at the Christmas Feast," said Carinna. "Please let me know what you will be contributing."

"I can make cupcakes," Ashley offered.

"The only thing I can make is Jell-O," Stephanie said.

"I can bake Christmas cookies," Shannen said, stretching the truth a little. Her mother used to bake cookies and Shannen was sure her mother would help.

"I'm not a good baker," Jonah said. "I'm a good taste-tester, though."

Shannen screwed up her nose and turned to face Jonah. "Fat chance I'm giving you any samples!"

"My dad's making moose pies," said Chris.

"Thanks, guys," Carinna replied. "And may I also remind everyone that in order to go on your trip, you must have more than fifty percent attendance," she added gently, as she counted heads in the class. Then she stuffed an old scarf into the gap below the door and began the day's lessons.

CHAPTER 2
The Old Ways

"Many young people have learned our cultural ways from elders who are passing the information on to the future. These elders have told us to use our Cree language every day and into the future so we can pass it on to our children."

Chelsea Edwards and Keisha Iahtail, 11, Attawapiskat, 2007

Watching the clock all day did not make the time go faster. Shannen tried to concentrate, but simmering feelings still threatened to boil over if anyone else mentioned the new school.

Finally, the end of the day came and Shannen greeted her cousins, Katrina and Ocean, with a forced smile. They joined the stream of kids heading home, sharing the wide streets with pick-up trucks, snowmobiles, and motley packs of half-wild dogs.

"I'm making cookies for the grad bake sale," Shannen said, as the girls passed by some of the reserve's small, boxy houses. Their boots crunched on the tidy blanket of snow winter had thrown over everything. "Let's look for recipes."

"You're so lucky, Shannen," Ocean said with a pout. "I wish I could go with you on the grad trip. I can't wait a whole year!"

"*Mahkah geegeesh*, Ocean. I have to wait two whole years!" Katrina cried.

"Well at least you'll be able to go to grade eight in a real school," Shannen blurted, sounding angrier than she had intended.

Katrina and Ocean were caught by surprise. Their cousin was usually all jokes and laughs on the walk home. "What's up with you, sister?" they asked in unison.

Shannen did not need much convincing to fill them in.

"...Then the other kids agreed with Jonah," Shannen said peevishly. She was tempted to call Jonah a jerk, but he and Katrina were cousins, so she bit her tongue. "I can't wait to see the look on Jonah's face when I prove him wrong."

The girls paused to look at a crèche that had been set up inside a tipi. "I think this house will win the prize for the best Christmas decorations," said Katrina, hoping the display would cheer up her cousin, who loved all things Christmas.

Shannen did brighten a little. "My dad decorated two big trees outside our house." Shannen thought Attawapiskat was the most beautiful at this time of year. The colored lights reflecting in the snow made every house look pretty.

Shannen greeted her husky dog, with kisses and scratches. As soon as she opened her front door, she knew that her great-grandmother was visiting. "Mmmm," the girls swooned, as the smell of warm fried bread came from the kitchen. The three girls kicked off their boots, added their coats to the heap inside the front door, and warmed their hands over the big, black wood stove that stood in the middle of the room.

"Hi-ho, Dallas!" Shannen squealed as she chased her little brother for a hug, darting in and out of a line of clothes that was hanging to dry. When Dallas was younger, "Hi-ho" was his saying for "I love you." Since then, "*Hi-ho mistahey*" ("I love you very much") was used a lot in the Koostachin home. "Is Serena home yet?"

"Not yet," mumbled Codee with her mouth full.

Shannen's husky was called Mahekun (pronounced Meekun), which means wolf in Cree.

"*Wacheyeh,* ShanShann," said Raven. Her eyes remained glued to the cartoons on the blaring television. "Mickiso is playing outside." Raven meant their younger brother, whose name means eagle in Cree.

Jaban hobbled toward the girls with a plate piled high with fist-sized balls of ragged dough. "Hi-ho mistahey, Jaban," Shannen said and kissed her great-grandmother's round cheeks, soft as satin pillows. "*Meegwetch.* We're starving."

"You make the best bannock in Attawapiskat, Jaban," Shannen said, bouncing the hot bread on her icy cold fingers. She pulled apart the crispy golden crust. The dough inside was soft and steamy. She wanted to slather it with jam, but that was a luxury. Food was very expensive on the reserve because everything was flown in. Shannen knew her family was lucky because her parents worked and could afford to buy more food than other families who relied on money from government. Even so, it was difficult to keep enough food in the house to feed seven kids.

"I wish we could make it this good," said Ocean.

"It takes time to learn to do something well," Jaban said in Cree, "And patience."

It looked so easy when Jaban made bannock. The girls watched her pour flour from a large yellow bag into the mixing bowl, and add pinches of salt, handfuls of sugar, and spoonfuls of baking powder. "We like it with raisins," they sometimes reminded her, hoping for a special treat. After mixing in the lard with her nimble fingertips, Jaban poured in some milk. She kneaded the dough and let it sit. Then she dropped spoonfuls of dough into hot oil. When the dumplings rose to the top, she turned them over and then they were ready. Whenever Shannen made the dough, it was either too sticky or too dry; the texture was never just right—and flour always ended up everywhere. Jaban just smiled. Shannen thought it would be easier to follow a recipe, but she knew it was important for her culture to learn how to do things in the old ways.

Shannen loved the traditional Cree foods her jaban cooked— boiled rabbit with tender dumplings, salted fish, such as cisco, walleye, and pike, and especially goose, smoked over a fire and

Chief James Kataquapit and his wife Janie and their children, George (far left) Marius, Celine (Kookum), David, Gabriel and Alex, in the 1940s

served with cranberries. After the men hunted the geese each spring, the girls helped take off the feathers. "Pluck, pluck, pluck—it's so boring, Jaban," Shannen had whined last time.

"Are you complaining, my great-granddaughter? I've been doing this since I was four years old, me," Jaban said, waving a crooked finger. "Children back in the old days had so many chores. We chopped wood to cook our food and heat our home.

Shannen found it boring to pluck geese,
but she liked being with her great-grandmother.

All day we collected bucket after bucket of snow to melt."
Shannen loved listening to these stories. "Life was hard back
then, especially when animals were scarce. There were no gro-
cery stores. You children don't know how easy life is for you."

It was true. Shannen could not imagine life without electricity and running water. Living in a tipi was fun when they
camped, but not all year round. And snowmobiles seemed way
easier than dog sleds and snowshoes.

"There were no refrigerators when I was a child either,"
Jaban told the girls. "Our families set up camp in the summer
to preserve food for the winter ahead. Back then there were so
many fish, when the men pulled in the nets, all the fish swim-
ming around looked like boiling water! My father came home
with his canoe filled to the brim. Now there are fewer fish. And
the government says we shouldn't eat too many because of mer-
cury poison." She sighed, creasing the deep worry lines between
her eyes. "People should know better than to contaminate the
land. It is the land that gives us life."

"When my mama sent me into the bush with a tin pail to
pick blueberries, I was always afraid of meeting bears, me—
especially polar bears," she said, lowering her voice. "They loved
berries as much as we did."

Wide-eyed, the children asked, "Did bears chase you, Jaban?"

Jaban laughed, her eyes crinkling into crescent moons.

"That's how I learned to run fast!" Shannen could not imagine Jaban doing anything fast, especially running.

When the girls finished their snack, Shannen reached for an old cookbook with a torn binding. Ocean found cookie recipes on pages that had been glued together with dried batter. Shannen pulled out a rolling pin and beaters from the junk drawer. She beamed, holding up star-shaped cookie cutters. "My mum used these to make cookies at Christmas before she starting working."

After they looked through the recipes, Ocean and Katrina bundled up to go home for their supper. Shannen craned her neck out of the door, wondering why Serena was so late. But just as she did, she caught sight of her sister walking with Julius and her parents silhouetted against butterscotch light where the sky met the land.

When her father come through the door Shannen could tell something was wrong. His smile always lit up the room, especially when Codee and Dallas threw themselves around each leg. But his face wore a worried look now. Then Shannen noticed Serena's puffy red eyes.

"I just had a talk with your grandfather about the school," her father said, solemnly. "It looks like we won't be getting a new one after all."

Wawatay News   FEBRUARY 7, 2008   ᐊᐧᐁᐧᑌ ᐊᐧᒋᐧᐁᐊᐧᐣ   **B 11**

No new school for Attawapiskat students

Lenny Carpenter
Wawatay News

The people of Attawapiskat feel "misled" and "betrayed" after learning Indian and Northern Affairs Canada (INAC) would not fund the construction of a new elementary school for at least another five years.

A week before Christmas, the community council learned INAC would not soon be funding the proposed $30-million school.

INAC spokesman Tony Prudori said due to "funding pressures," INAC had to review its budget. The department decided funding the construction of the school is "not on our long-term capital plan," he said.

In a news conference Jan. 24, Mushkegowuk Grand Chief Stan Louttit said the community feels "betrayed" and "lied to," since INAC promised funding for a new school in 2005.

"We find this very appalling," Louttit said.

"Why should people have to put up with this? Going to a proper school is a right for every Canadian, Native or non-Native."

Prudori said providing education is still a priority for INAC, and that it provided $3 million to construct portables when the J.R. Nakogee School was forced to close eight years ago. The school closed after students reported being sick and their illnesses were linked to a diesel fuel spill on the school property 15 years prior.

INAC also provided $250,000 to modify the local high school so it could accommodate some elementary students.

Although Prudori said a Health Canada inspection determined the portables did not pose any immediate health or safety concerns, school principal Stella Wesley disagreed.

Wesley said the portables endanger the students' health and learning.

She described each portable as "drafty." The air is cold when students enter class in the morning.

To attend gym class, each student must put on winter clothes and walk up to 700 feet to the community gymnasium, and afterwards walk back to class in -40 C temperatures while covered in sweat.

Paint and wood are starting to peel and crack.

There are fire safety concerns, as the doors tend to jam and each portable is overcrowded with more than 40 students and teaching staff. Each portable is supposed to last 10 years, but Wesley said "I don't think they'll last that long."

This year, more than 400 students ranging from junior kindergarten to Grade 8 attend classes in the portables.

In five years, school officials project Attawapiskat will have 640 elementary students.

Steve Hookimaw, chairman of the Attawapiskat First Nation Education Authority, said the authority secured a loan to start construction and just needs a tuition agreement from INAC before proceeding.

"Eight years is too long," he said. "We need a new school.

"Our children are not different from other (Canadian) children."

The community will continue to lobby and attempt to re-enter negotiations with INAC.

CHAPTER 3
Keep Walking in Your Moccasins

"How can he tell us that we don't have the right to a new school? All students in Canada deserve a learning environment that they are proud to attend, and that gives them hope. We want the same hope as every other Canadian student."

Shannen Koostachin, 13, 2008

"No school?" bellowed Shannen, in disbelief. "But the minister made a promise!"

"Yes, *danis*, but a new Indian Affairs minister cancelled the plans," her father explained. "He said it wasn't a priority."

"Not a priority!" Shannen stomped her foot and shouted, "How can he say that? Has he ever seen our portables? The mould? The cracks in the walls?"

"They say they don't have the money right now," her father replied, trying his best to keep calm.

Serena began to cry. Shannen cradled her arm around her older sister's quaking shoulders.

"How can a new minister break promises made by two other ministers?" Serena asked between sobs, angrily slapping the couch cushion. "How can one politician wreck our future?" Now Codee and Dallas were crying, too. They were not used to seeing their big sister so upset.

"The government is responsible for over six hundred reserve schools," said her mother, scooping up Dallas in a hug. "Your mooshoom knows of at least forty that need replacing. One school burned down. Another is infested with snakes."

The Koostachin Bunch

(From left) Shannen's mother, Jenny Nakogee,
Julius, Mickiso, Serena, Shannen, Codee, Raven, Dallas,
and Shannen's dad, Andrew Koostachin

"But it's not fair!" yelled Shannen, even louder. "The government should build a school for every reserve that needs one."

"Yeah, isn't that our treaty right?" asked her older brother, Julius, bitterly. He was referring to the James Bay Treaty signed by his ancestors. "No matter what we do, the government will break promises like they always have. Nothing will ever change."

Serena lifted her head and nodded. "Ever right, Julius. I'll never trust any politician."

Jonah's words hammered in Shannen's ears. We're not getting a new school.

Shannen narrowed her eyes into an icy stare. "They broke their promise because we're Indians," she said through clenched teeth, "because we don't count for anything." Her parents had always taught her to be proud of their Cree heritage. The government sure didn't make it easy. How could she face everyone tomorrow?

"I know that this is terribly disappointing news," her father said, placing his arm around his wife's shoulder. "But we have always taught you children to be strong." He paused to look each of them in the eye. "And never to give up."

Shannen could tell by the way Serena avoided her father's eyes that her sister had already given up. "But, Papa. It's impossible!" Shannen cried.

"Nothing is impossible," her father continued. "If you believe in something, stand up and speak for what you believe."

Shannen felt her bruised heart swell with love as the tears choked in her throat. Her dad had a gentle way of turning a bad situation around to be hopeful. He taught his children to respect the Seven Grandfathers—Love, Respect, Truth, Honesty, Humility, Bravery, and Wisdom. They stood behind them, giving support at all times. "Take three steps in life," he told them, "Put the Creator first, because He made you and me; second is family, because they give you love; the third is education." Andrew Koostachin was respected as a good and strong leader, and at times like this, Shannen understood why.

"I know that today you feel all hope for a new school is gone, but tomorrow I want you to get up, pick up your books, and keep walking in your moccasins."

CHAPTER 4
We Won't Give Up

"These children are beautiful people; they have ideas, skills, and abilities which need to be encouraged and inspired as much as any other child in Canada. We need to provide them with a place where they are proud to go every day."

Carinna Pellett, elementary school teacher, Attawapiskat, 2008

"*Esh kah ken-oygoh.* Wake up now," Shannen's mother yelled down the hall.

Shannen moaned, "*Moonah!*" and wrapped her blankets around her like a cocoon.

For the first few seconds after she awoke, Shannen thought the news about the school was just a bad dream. Then the truth flooded over her like a cold, wet wave.

It had taken her a long time to fall asleep. It wasn't just hearing Serena's muffled crying. Shannen could not control the fierce anger in her heart. Her little brothers and sisters and cousins had a right to the same education as any other kid in

Canada. School is a time for hopes and dreams, she kept thinking. Every kid deserves that!

"Get up, ShanShann!" Serena clucked, just like her mother. "There's only one day left before the holidays." Shannen couldn't understand how it was possible for Serena to be so responsible.

Shannen hoped to slip into the portable quietly, but of course the door was stuck and she had to shove it to get in. In one glance, Shannen could tell that the kids were talking about the broken promise.

"Ho-ho-ho! Some Christmas present, eh Shannen?" Chris said sarcastically.

Shannen's stomach churned as she waited for Jonah's I-told-you-so remarks. But no one said anything more.

Instead of starting the day's lessons, Carinna sat on one of the desks beside the group. "I know everyone is disappointed to hear this news," Carinna said. "It is so unfair." Shannen detected a tremble in the teacher's voice. "When I first came here, I was shocked. Last year, I worked in Kiribati in the Pacific Ocean." Carinna grabbed a globe from a nearby shelf and pointed to the scattered chain of islands. "I expected poor living conditions there because I knew it was a very poor country." Carinna wrapped her coat around her tightly. "But there is no excuse for such conditions in Canada."

Shannen cringed. Would Carinna leave like all the other teachers who hated teaching in portables? All the kids liked Carinna Pellett, which was not true of many teachers who came to the north. And Carinna's students knew that she liked them, too.

Shannen looked around at her classmates. They still said nothing. She had been dreading their reactions, but in the end, it was the fact that no one said anything that bothered her. It was as if they weren't even angry, as if they had just accepted it.

Even though all signs were pointing the other way, deep inside Shannen did not want to let go of the dream for a new school. She wanted better things for all the children of Attawapiskat. She wanted Serena's efforts to mean something.

"I don't think we should give up yet!" The words just tumbled out.

Then came the voice Shannen had been dreading the most. "You're crazy!" Jonah snorted. "What else can we do? We wrote useless letters. Serena even went to Ottawa."

Shannen didn't have an answer yet.

"Jonah's right. It's impossible!" said Chris, echoing Shannen's own thoughts from the night before.

"Nothing's impossible," Shannen said, boldly, though inside she was still working on convincing herself.

"We're just kids, Shannen. Kids don't have any power," Solomon said. "We're too young to vote. Why should any politician pay attention to us?"

"Face facts, Shannen. No one is gonna listen to us, no matter what we do. When will you get it?" said Jonah wearily, as if she had no sense at all. "The government just doesn't care!"

Shannen happened to know that wasn't exactly true. "What about Charlie? He's in the government. He listens. He cares." When Serena had gone to Ottawa she met Charlie Angus, who represented their large riding of Timmins/James Bay. Everyone could tell that he was genuinely concerned about the First Nations. Serena also thought Charlie was pretty cool because he sang and played guitar in a rock band.

Carinna jumped in. "The principal says our literacy levels are down. Attendance is down, too."

"School is boring," said Brendon. "During our break we mostly just stand around. We don't have a playground, or a gym. Our library isn't really a library, it's just a bunch of books in a pile."

Emma said, "Playing at recess is dangerous with all the ice and snow. Kids skipping and kicking balls are always wiping out and there's not enough room to run around."

Shannen detected a spark of interest catching. She joined in. "My dad asked a boy who dropped out of school in grade five why he stopped attending. He answered, 'Because it's not a real school anyway; it's just buildings scattered all over.'"

"Yeah. Our school is like the trailer park of education," muttered Jonah.

"Hey, good one, brother!" Solomon laughed.

Chris spoke next, slowly collecting his thoughts. "I feel sorry for all the little kids who will have to spend their school years in crappy portables, like we did."

Ashley was the first to back Shannen up. "Maybe Shannen's right. Maybe we should try one more time."

Jonah rolled his eyes, but Shannen ignored him. "Maybe we

Children play outside the portables in the J.R. Nakogee schoolyard.

can mount a new Students-Helping-Students campaign," she said. "A bigger and better one."

"No one will pay attention to stupid letters," Jonah grumbled.

"What about setting up a website?" Chris suggested. "We could ask people to sign a petition telling the government that their decision isn't fair."

"Or maybe we should go on strike. That might get Ottawa's attention," Jonah said. He laughed, but Shannen could tell that he was only half joking.

"That's a terrific idea, Jonah!" Shannen exclaimed, "We can make signs and walk around the portables."

"I can help make signs," Brendon volunteered. Several other students offered, too.

"We can scream and yell," Solomon said.

"WE WANT A NEW SCHOOL!" shouted Ashley and Stephanie.

Then the whole class chanted, "WE WANT A NEW SCHOOL! WE WANT A NEW SCHOOL!"

"I think this is a great suggestion," said Carinna, enthusiastically. "We'll need to speak to the principal to see if she supports the idea."

Shannen's heart raced. "Maybe the whole school can go on strike," she said excitedly, her eyes sparkling. "And we won't give up until we have justice for the children of Attawapiskat!"

CHAPTER 5
The Circle Is Strong

"I support the other students who are non-Natives. I would help them as well. This is why we are made in the circle. One part of the circle is red, one is yellow, the other is white and the other is black. We are all the same."

Shannen Koostachin, 13, 2008

After school, Shannen and Katrina met Ocean and some other grade seven friends, Chelsea and Keisha, for a dodgeball game at the arena. Shannen was bursting with energy —more than usual—and she could not stop chattering about the new campaign.

"I'll ask our class, too," Chelsea said. "I just know they'll want to join in."

When she arrived home, Shannen exploded through the front door and proudly delivered the news. She danced around her family members, who were seated in front of the television.

Her parents exchanged smiles. "You were probably too young

to remember when the whole community protested outside the old school back in 2000," her father said. "Everyone carried signs, even the little kids. The parents brought hammers and boards and nailed them to the windows and doors. Then we went over to picket in front of the band office."

Shannen was eager to hear more.

"We sent photos to some newspapers down south," continued her father. "After the story was published, the government finally admitted that the school was contaminated. The school was condemned and they promised to build another. That's when the construction trailers were brought in as temporary classrooms."

"When did the Students-Helping-Students campaign begin?" Shannen asked Serena, hoping her sister might offer to help.

In 2000, the community made signs and protested about the contamination of J.R. Nakogee School.

"That was later—a grade five class in Iroquois Falls learned that the government had broken their promise to build a permanent school and the kids got really upset."

"One girl banged her fist on the desk and said, 'That's not right!'" added her mother. "Her name was Justice—perfect, eh?"

"The students didn't see this as a First Nations injustice," Serena continued. "They felt all children should have a good school, no matter who they were or where they lived in Canada."

Shannen was eating everything up except her dinner. "Shannen, you are letting your soup get cold!" her mother scolded.

Shannen ate a spoonful of soup as her brother picked up the story. "Those students couldn't imagine what it was like not having a building where everyone could be together," Julius said. He was old enough to remember the old school. "I never liked school in the same way after we moved to the portables."

"The teacher suggested writing letters," Serena added, spooning the last mouthfuls of soup into Dallas, "to tell the government it wasn't fair that the kids in Attawapiskat didn't have a decent education."

Her father added, "These children understood what the politicians didn't." He quoted one of his favorite sayings, "Out of the mouths of babes…"

Shannen said, "Solomon thinks that politicians don't pay any attention to kids."

Serena shook her head. "I think politicians paid more attention to the letters because they were from kids." Shannen thought she saw a glint of interest in Serena's eyes—maybe she had not given up after all. Shannen decided that being too pushy might backfire, so she kept her thoughts to herself.

By the next day, the news of the broken promise had traveled across Attawapiskat. The school and band office were getting phone calls from angry parents. "We'll talk about it at the Christmas Feast when the whole town will be there," said Shannen's father. Shannen's eyes flashed at the thought of her entire community getting involved again.

Before the Feast, Shannen's father hitched up the large wooden sleigh to their snowmobile for the annual Christmas parade. Families decorated 'floats' with everything from wrapping paper to trees, caribou skins, antlers, and tipis. Santa was in the lead pickup truck. Following behind was a long line of snowmobiles and vans. There were so many people in the parade that there was hardly anyone lining the roads to watch. Later, the Koostachin family went to the Feast with a large pot of moose

A Christmas
Parade in
Attawapiskat

stew, potato chips, and pop. The Reg Louttit Sportsplex looked festive with snow sculptures and a large decorated tree outside the entrance.

Shannen was bouncing around more than usual, anxious to know what people had to say about the campaign. "What if the community has given up, too?" she asked her father.

"There's no point in worrying about 'what ifs.' You might waste time worrying about an 'if' that never happens. You must have faith, daughter!"

Dallas and Codee joined the other rosy-cheeked children chasing each other around the gymnasium, playing hide-and-seek under the long tables where the food was placed, and grabbing fistfuls of snacks. Shannen offered to get coffee or tea bloss for several of the elders while she waited for them to start talking about the school.

The school principal was the first to raise the subject. "I am sick and tired of waiting for a solution to this problem. The oil leak was almost thirty years ago. My students don't want to wait any longer. They want to protest the government's decision."

The Deputy Chief agreed. "Like many of you, I was taken away from my parents when I reached school age and forced to attend school far away in the south," she said. "The deep sorrow caused by this residential school experience remains in each generation. Now our children are still experiencing an inferior education system. This is not right!"

Katrina's mother stood with one hand in the small of her back and the other on the side of her pregnant belly. "It's not just the portables that are a problem. The kids are still breathing fumes from the contaminated site. My Rob has asthma, eczema, and heart problems," Rosie said, lifting the hand of her youngest. "I love children. They make life wonderful. Why doesn't the government tear down the old school and clean up the site for the sake of the children?"

"It's not right to have children breathing polluted air!" Shannen's father declared. "It's not right that schools funded by the province have higher standards, more money, smaller class sizes, and safer buildings than schools funded by the federal government on the reserves. Why is it different for students on reserves?"

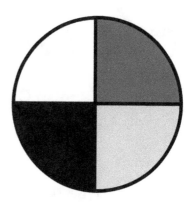

A Medicine Wheel

"In January, our National Chief is visiting Attawapiskat," said the Chief. The National Chief was the elected representative of the Assembly of First Nations and spoke for all Aboriginal Peoples in the country. "This is a good opportunity to protest the government's decision."

Then Shannen's grandfather, John B., asked everyone to come together and hold hands to form a large circle. "The circle is strong. This is why we are made in the circle. The circle is an important principle in our Aboriginal beliefs. The circle has no beginning and no end. We are all connected. No one is in front of us, behind us, above us, or below us. Together we keep the circle strong!"

As John B. gave a blessing for the food they were about to eat, Shannen closed her eyes and silently thanked each elder who was standing up for the rights of children. Shannen felt the spirit of her loved ones and the wisdom of her ancestors flow through the unending circle. Together we keep the circle strong!

CHAPTER 6
We Are Important, Too!

"It really feels like we're alone and that no one cares. But we really think we can make a difference."

Shannen Koostachin, 13, 2008

"No wind, Serena," Shannen said, yawning as she looked out of her bedroom window. "It's a perfect day for a protest."

Finally, it was the day of the National Chief's visit. Shannen had been worried about their beautiful new signs blowing away. She enjoyed most things about winter, but disliked the wind, which could be ferocious. The scantily dressed spruce trees on the horizon were very poor buffers.

Once she'd shaken off her sleepiness, Shannen began fluttering around the kitchen table. "We're going to picket at lunchtime," she said. "Rosie will take photos to send to the government and to the newspapers down south."

"Sit down and eat, Shannen," her mother said.

Raven asked, "Do we strike all afternoon?"

"I don't know," Shannen said. "I've never been on a picket line before."

"Will we get to eat our lunch?" Mickiso wondered.

Shannen tousled his hair. "Is that all you think about?"

"Mama, I want to pick-a-line, too," cried Dallas.

"But you're only in nursery school," said Codee. "You're too young."

Their mother cut in. "No one is going to be left out. We can all pick-a-line."

At noon, the students piled out of the portables carrying the signs each class had made. Flakes like downy Snow goose feathers swirled around the children as they stomped up and down in front of the portables yelling, "We Need a New School!"

Then the group marched the short distance to the band office. "That must be the National Chief," said Shannen, pointing to the white-haired man who was standing on the steps of the bright blue building.

"I'm proud to see young, Aboriginal Peoples standing up and speaking out for their right to a decent school," he shouted

Even young children took part in protesting for a new school, in January, 2008.

through a megaphone. "Canadians should be aware of this situation. Canadians don't know what is happening here. They don't know that kids are being mistreated."

A few days later, Shannen's father casually announced at dinner, "Our Member of Parliament is coming to Attawapiskat."

"Really?" screeched Shannen, leaping up. "Why didn't you tell me?"

"I just did," he replied, laughing. "After seeing photos of kids at the protest, he decided to come to help us launch the campaign."

"Eh heh!" said Shannen, slapping the table. "Do you think he would visit our portables?"

"Why don't you e-mail him and ask?" replied her father.

A couple of weeks later, on the day of Charlie Angus's visit, Shannen was bubbling over with excitement. When she arrived at school, she tried to get her friends' attention but they were huddled around the bulletin board reading from travel brochures.

Stephanie, a big fan of horror movies, read out from a list of Niagara Falls attractions.

"...the House of Frankenstein, the Nightmare Fear Factory..."

Shannen was easily drawn into the discussion. She picked up a Canada's Wonderland brochure. "Test your level of thrill being spun 360 degrees on Riptide, free falling 230 feet on Drop Tower..."

"I want to go under the falls in the *Maid of the Mist*," Ashley interrupted, "but the Whirlpool Jet Tours sound awesome, too!"

"Although I'm thrilled to see you guys reading, I'm afraid I have to interrupt," Carinna said, firmly. "We have a very special guest this morning." She went on to prepare her students with a brief civics lesson. "Charlie Angus was elected to represent us in Parliament. Every elected Member of Parliament has a seat in the House of Commons—"

"My dad always says that all politicians do is sit around in Ottawa," joked Chris, setting off laughter through the room.

Carinna pressed on over her students' chuckles. "Each member belongs to a party—"

Solomon called out, "So they sit around *and* party? No wonder it's taking so long to get a new school!"

Carinna smiled and waited for the laughter to subside again.

"The party with the most seats is in power…"

Before she could finish, Charlie and the principal appeared at the door. Shannen's classmates were suddenly quiet and looked down at their desks. As Charlie scanned the room, Shannen wanted to explain to him that outsiders made the kids shy and uncomfortable.

"Wacheyeh," the politician said, in a friendly manner. Still, the kids stared at their desks.

"Tell me, if you and your father went out in the bush in winter, how long do you think you would survive?"

Shannen was surprised at the question but not surprised that her friends didn't answer. Carinna jumped in. "A long time," she said. She knew that each of her students was very experienced at hunting, fishing, and wilderness survival.

"Now, if I went out in the bush in this environment without anyone guiding me, how long do you think I would survive?" Ashley and Stephanie covered their mouths and giggled. Some other kids looked up. "A month?" Charlie asked. More kids laughed and shook their heads. "How about a week?"

The kids all looked at Brendon. He had the reputation of being the best hunter in the class. "Maybe a day, if you're lucky," Brendon called out.

Jonah muttered, "More like an hour."

"So, if you and your parents went to Parliament without a guide, how long do you think you'd survive?"

Now the kids were getting it.

"I'm here to help guide you in your campaign to get a new school," Charlie continued. "Changing attitudes and changing the way things are done is never easy, especially in the government." All eyes were now on Charlie.

"A decent education is a fundamental right for all Canadians," Charlie declared. "It's time to break down the walls of educational apartheid for First Nations students and treat all students as equals."

Carinna stood up and explained the word "apartheid"—the system of segregation between whites and blacks in South Africa.

"I have faith that when Canadians learn about Attawapiskat, they will hang their heads in shame," Charlie said. "They will not stand for it! The students of Attawapiskat deserve better."

All the students made signs for the protest.

CHAPTER 7
Stand By Me

"Canada is rich and we can't find enough to provide schools for the First Nations people? We were surprised and pretty shocked and disgusted by that."

Julien Dyer, Neil McNeil High School student, Toronto, 2008

Outside in the winter's gloom, a February storm was brewing, the nasty kind that tempted kids to stay at home. Inside the grade eight portable, the spark of interest in the Students-Helping-Students campaign, had ignited a flame. Kids who might otherwise have skipped school were showing up every day. Instead of starting each day moaning about the cold, Carinna encouraged the students to share their news about the latest developments.

"We were on CTV news!" she announced one morning. She went on to tell them about students in Toronto who were raising money to build schools in Africa until they heard about

Attawapiskat. "Now they want to do something to help."

Waving a newspaper over her head, Shannen blurted excitedly, "We're in the newspaper, too!" She read out, "Support is growing for the students of Attawapiskat. The Grade 5 class at St. Patrick's School in Cobalt, Ontario, has joined the fight for a new school in the First Nation." Shannen looked up from the newspaper, "Charlie was showing pictures of our portables to that class and one of the kids said, 'I'm going to put this on YouTube.' Charlie said that would never have occurred to him in a million years, but it gave him the idea to make his own video! Kids teaching politicians—how cool is that!"

She continued reading, "The class is joining the Students-Helping-Students letter-writing campaign to call on the federal government to live up to its commitment to build a grade school in the remote community." Shannen added. "Schools from all over Ontario have written letters to the government—and not just students—teachers, too." Then she held up some cards with hand-drawn pictures. "They're even sending us letters and cards."

"People are also signing the petition on our new website," said Chris. "It has information about the campaign and links to Facebook pages and blogs."

"There's a link to Charlie's YouTube video," Shannen said.

"Can we see it?" a bunch of them asked. Carinna groaned

Shannen holds up postcards the Attawapiskat children received in the Students-Helping-Students campaign, 2008.

about going back outside into the blowing snow to walk to the portable where they had Internet access, but Shannen could tell that she was just as excited as her students.

As images of their reserve and their school appeared on the screen, the kids stared, wide-eyed.

"Holay! People all over the world will finally see our crappy portables," Jonah cried.

The students called out the names of the children they recognized in the pictures, drowning out John Lennon's version of "Stand By Me" that played the whole video through. They booed when a blurry image of the minister sitting in a red stagecoach wearing a cowboy hat came on screen.

Chris snorted. "Figures they'd put a cowboy in charge of Indian Affairs!"

Then, for the first time, the students saw in clear focus the person with the power to give them a school. He looked so normal.

"I can't see his horns and tail," said Jonah, moving forward and peering closely at the screen.

"Get out of the way!" the others yelled.

In three minutes, the whole story of J.R. Nakogee school was given in simple words and images, from the children holding up protest signs in 2000 to the last broken promise. The video explained that Native children are denied the same education rights that are guaranteed to other Canadian children. Then it said, "The children are fighting back. They have launched a campaign for a new school. They are writing letters. They are saying that educational apartheid must end. Canadians should hide their heads in shame. The students of Attawapiskat deserve better."

The class erupted in cheers.

The video ended with a message to write to the minister in Ottawa.

After they had watched the video several times, Shannen asked Carinna, "Can we see the one of Charlie and the minister?" She said to her classmates, "They're talking about us in Ottawa!"

"Shannen is referring to Question Period," Carinna explained. "Members like Charlie, who are not in the governing party, can ask questions of the ministers in charge of departments, such as Indian Affairs." Carinna found the link and pressed play.

"Mr. Speaker, the families of Attawapiskat are reeling because a school for which they have fought for eight years has been cancelled," Charlie said angrily.

At the mention of their reserve, the portable got dead quiet. Politicians on screen banged their desks and yelled out, "Shame! Shame!" Shannen looked around at the stunned looks on the faces of her classmates.

The minister responded, "Mr. Speaker, there are no health concerns in that school."

"No health concerns?" Chris talked back to the screen. "Then how'd you like to send your own kids here?"

The politicians' exchange became louder and angrier. They pointed fingers and threw down papers.

"Don't you children get any ideas," Carinna warned with a smile.

"Yeah, we'd be kicked out for sure!" Jonah said, snickering.

As they walked back to their portable, the blowing snow pricked Shannen's face like shards of glass. While the others mimicked the politicians, yelling, "Shame! Shame!" Shannen was thinking about all the people who were standing together

The cold of January didn't stop the children from protesting in 2008.

to help them—students, politicians, school boards, churches, teachers' associations. Working together was making a difference. Shannen could feel hope growing as the words of the song on the video played over and over in her mind. "No I won't be afraid, no I won't shed a tear, just as long as you stand, stand by me."

School boards join reserve fight

Ontario students encouraged to write letters calling for funds to build school for Attawapiskat children

LOUISE BROWN
EDUCATION REPORTER

They sit scattered in portables so run down the James Bay wind can blow through cracks in the wall. Twice this winter pipes have frozen, leaving students nowhere to go but home.

It has been eight years since parents in Attawapiskat, in Ontario's northern woodland, pulled their children out of the town's grade school because of contaminated soil and moved them to what they thought would be temporary portables. But the 400 students still suit up in boots and coats every time they visit the school library, computer room or special education class or the town gym — then do it all over again when they head back to class.

So poor is this setting for learning, it's no wonder some children here drop out by Grade 8, says Attawapiskat principal Stella Wesley.

"Portables aren't the whole problem, but they make children feel very isolated in a community already segregated from the rest of society," said Wesley, whose stu-

dents are at the heart of a national push for federal funding for a new school.

Ontario's public school boards will encourage their 2.1 million students to write letters to the federal department of Indian and Northern Affairs to urge funding for a new school in this northern Cree community, after eight years of waiting for funding from successive federal governments.

Several schools plan to lead a student awareness campaign for Attawapiskat, including Toronto's Neil McNeil Catholic Secondary School and The Student School, a public alternative school.

"All children have the right to a quality education, and we want the students of Attawapiskat to know their peers care about them," said Waterloo trustee Catherine Fife, vice-president of the Ontario Public School Boards' Association.

The boards are responding to NDP MP Charlie Angus' YouTube call for the public to push Indian Affairs Minister Chuck Strahl for funds for a new school in Attawapiskat, to replace the one contam-

RICHARD LAUTENS/TORONTO STAR

Residents of Attawapiskat, a community in northern Ontario, have been fighting for a school to house 400 students now in rundown portables. Two Toronto schools plan to lead an awareness campaign on the issue.

inated in 1979 by a toxic diesel spill.

An Indian Affairs spokesperson told the *Star* this week there are no plans or timetables for when a new school might be built in Attawapiskat, even though government officials had said last fall one was in the works.

But federal officials say an unexpected fire in another native community meant having to replace it at a cost of $13 million, pushing the

Attawapiskat school off the current waiting list.

"There's not a single other school in the country that is made up entirely of portables with no main building. It's unacceptable in the 21st century, especially given the dropout rate among First Nations children," said Angus, whose riding of Timmins-James Bay includes the struggling fly-in reserve.

Ontario's public school boards' as-

sociation has cited aboriginal learning as a top priority and launched a number of initiatives to try to close the learning gap between native and non-native children.

"We've reached a new low in Ontario if a community like this is not even on a waiting list for a new school," said Fife.

Information on the campaign for a new school is at www.attawapiskatschool.com.

CHAPTER 8
Eight Long Years

"WE ARE ALL THE SAME. Please don't ignore us because we're different."

Shannen Koostachin, 13, 2008

"Stop climbing the snow piles. You'll get soaking wet," shouted Shannen, trying to herd her younger brothers and sisters to school and get them there dry and on time. Although the spring thaw had finally begun, most of the ground was still covered with snow. The warm sun drew kids outside to ride their bikes through muddy ruts, play road hockey, and carve hopscotch courts in patches of gravel.

"I wish I could be there when you show your video," Raven said, kicking a piece of ice.

"Maybe you'll make movies when you grow up," Mickiso said.

"No, I'm going to be a politician like Charlie. I could be the first Aboriginal Minister of Indian Affairs—then every Native child would have a good school," Shannen replied. "Or, how does this sound? The Right Honorable Shannen Koostachin, Prime Minister of Canada."

"I like it!" Raven said as she gave Shannen a fistbump.

When the kids in Shannen's class were settled at their desks, Carinna started the day's announcements. "I know you all want to talk about the campaign, but we also need to discuss some grad trip fundraising events. Ashley?"

"We're having another bake sale at the arena during the hockey tournament," said Ashley, holding up a shocking pink Bristol board sign announcing the date, time, and a list of foods—chili and bannock, moose pies, and boiled raisin pudding.

"There's another casino night," added Shannen. "We need more prizes, though. Someone has already offered a chainsaw and a cord of wood for the raffle."

"Of course we also need to come to a decision about our destination," said Carinna. The debates on whether to go to Toronto or Niagara Falls had been getting more and more heated.

"We could see a Toronto Raptors' game in Toronto," said Chris, who had a dream of playing basketball professionally.

"And we could go to the Hockey Hall of Fame!" said Brendon,

a star player for the Akimiski Islanders. "I want to see where my Number 22 sweater's going to be one day."

Solomon said, "I want to see the dinosaur bones at the Royal Ontario Museum."

Jonah argued, "The Science Centre is way better."

"I want to go under the falls in the *Maid of the Mist*," Ashley interrupted.

"You guys can get all the thrills you need at Canada's Wonderland," Shannen argued.

"I know of a great camp," said Carinna.

Camp? Shannen cringed for her teacher. The Cree kids knew all about camp. They went to camps on weekends and summer holidays. For two weeks in April, they had "Goose Break," when families left Attawapiskat to hunt geese.

"We can camp any old time," groaned Solomon.

"Sleeping in tents? Ugh!" said Stephanie, screwing up her nose behind her hand so their teacher could not see.

Shannen didn't want to hurt her teacher's feelings, but she was looking forward to clean, white, hotel sheets and soft feather pillows—and shopping.

"You don't have to sleep in tents at Camp Wenonah, there are cabins. There's rock-climbing, and kayaking—all sorts of different activities. Muskoka is beautiful. You will love it," said Carinna.

"But, Carinna, will we still have enough time to look for our grad dresses?" Ashley asked, setting off a chain reaction of panic among the girls. They had saved up all year to buy their grad dresses. Attawapiskat was definitely not the Paris of the North when it came to fashion.

"My mother's making me buy a suit at one of the factory outlet malls," Jonah groaned, followed by several similar admissions from the boys.

"You're kidding, right? You'd rather shop than kayak and rock-climb?" asked Brendon.

Niagara Falls, with its Great Canadian Midway,
was one of the choices for the grad trip.

Carinna thought about this and said, "You know, Niagara Falls and Toronto are less than two hours apart. And Canada's Wonderland is just north of Toronto. We could spend a few days in each and stop by Camp Wenonah on the way home. That should give you plenty of time to shop. So...? Who votes yes?"

All hands went up, eventually. The verdict was in. Niagara Falls, Toronto, Canada's Wonderland, and Camp Wenonah. Everybody was happy.

Next, Carinna winked at Shannen and announced, "I brought my laptop today so we can watch Shannen's video." Shannen squirmed in her chair. She was even more nervous because the principal had been invited. But Shannen was pleased with her project. She had worked hard to learn the software, write the script, and collect all the photos—kids carrying homemade signs, close-ups of the cracks in the walls and doors, and the bathroom. She even wrote a poem.

Ministers
I made a poem just for you
I did it 'cause WE WANT A SCHOOL
We really hope you change your mind
Even ministers like you should be kind
Eight long years we've been waiting
Our hope was strong but now it's fading

How could you bring us down to a lie?
We had our smiles up, but brought down to a sigh
Please, we don't want to wait again
It's time for you to stand up and be a man!

When the video ended, Ashley flung her arms around Shannen. "I knew you could do it! This is awesome."

"I hope the jerks in Ottawa watch it and weep!" Chris said.

"Maybe they'll finally come and see our portables," Jonah added, giving Shannen a playful punch. "Shannen, this video rocks!"

Shannen beamed.

Afterwards, the principal made an exciting announcement. "Peetabeck Academy is organizing an education rally in support of our school campaign." Shannen knew about the new school in Fort Albany. It was about 155 miles (250 km) away, the envy of all the James Bay communities. "They will light a Sacred Fire on the first day and keep it lit for four days as we do in our culture during times of need."

Shannen was thrilled. "Imagine!" she cried. "They have a beautiful new school and they are helping us get one, too."

"On the fourth day, other schools across the province will light candles and pray for guidance and strength to show unity with our community," the principal continued.

"Can we go?" Shannen asked excitedly.

"Sure—if your families give permission," the principal answered.

Carinna said, "This is a wonderful opportunity."

Later, Carinna gave out an assignment for each student to write a speech. "We'll pick three or four to read in Fort Albany," she said. Shannen thought about Serena's "Forgotten Children of Attawapiskat" speech, and wondered if she could write anything even close to as good.

That evening, as she set the table, Shannen chattered cheerfully about the rally. "Katrina's whole family is coming to dance," she told her mother. Shannen spread her arms and twirled as if she was Fancy Shawl dancing.

"That sounds like fun, Shannen. I'd like to go, too," said her mother, putting a pan of lasagna in the oven to keep warm for Mickiso and Raven who were still outside playing.

Her father added, "We could drive you on the winter ice road." The road down the coast was only open between January and March.

Serena asked brightly, "Me, too?" Shannen tried to hide her smile. Serena was definitely showing more interest.

Their mother said, "I'm sorry, danis. If your father and I go to Fort Albany, we will need you to mind your brothers and sisters."

"Why can't Julius do it?" Serena protested, even though it was futile. Julius had lots of hockey practices at this time of year.

Serena turned to Shannen. "I hope your speech gets picked. You'd be a great speaker. You aren't shy like me."

"I could never write a speech as good as yours," she said.

"You can do it, ShanShann," said Serena, sweetly. Shannen pulled a face so pathetic that Serena had to laugh. "Of course I'll help you, brat!"

That night, Serena helped Shannen get started. "First, write down all the things you don't like about the portables. Then write down how the conditions make you feel." This part was easy. It did not take long for Shannen to write several pages. "Now, write it as if you were talking. Then take out everything that you don't need," Serena suggested. "People don't like long, boring speeches."

"I wish you could come to Fort Albany, Serena," said Shannen. "I'll be so nervous to read my speech."

"I was nervous, too. But when I realized that I wasn't speaking for myself—I was speaking for all the children of Attawapiskat—that gave me courage." Serena yawned. "You'll be fine, as long as you are standing up for what you believe. Hi-ho mistahey, ShanShann."

CHAPTER 9
Sacred Fire

"I wish I had my life to live over so I would know what it feels like to go to a school like this."

Shannen Koostachin, 13, 2008

Shannen pressed her nose to the window as her father pulled up in front of Peetabeck Academy.

"Omigawd! What an awesome school!" Shannen leapt out and ran across the lawn for a better view. Suspended over a wide circle of stones, was a dreamcatcher. Below was the Sacred Fire, tended by the Fire Keeper who was responsible for keeping the flames lit day and night. Over the front entrance of the school was an enormous carved goose head of Aboriginal design. When she walked through the doors, the first thing Shannen noticed was the blast of heat. "It's so warm," she swooned.

"Wacheyeh, Shannen!" She turned to see Charlie Angus with a small group of elders.

"Hey, man!" Shannen waved, grinning.

"We're just about to have a tour. Would you like to join us?" The group from Attawapiskat jumped at the chance.

Shannen craned her neck up, down, and around as they walked along wide, polished corridors. The high walls were decorated with beautiful Native artwork. Lockers were painted in cheerful bright colors. An open door welcomed Shannen into a fresh, clean, light-filled classroom. She looked longingly at all the bookshelves lining the walls, ran her fingers along the plastic tubs of pencils, erasers and glue sticks, pads of paper, crayons and markers used to make the cheerful art that plastered the classroom walls. Shannen loved to draw but J.R. Nakogee didn't have many supplies, or teachers who knew much about art.

As Shannen moved from room to room, her enjoyment turned to something else. The stories and poems, math work, and science fair projects were so much more advanced than what she was learning. Each class even had a computer! A cloud of gloom darkened Shannen's spirit. Suddenly the thought of attending Vezina High School gave her a sick feeling.

Suddenly chanting pierced the air. Shannen joined the stream of people heading to the gymnasium entrance where her friends were waiting. As soon they stepped through the doors, the darkness that had enveloped her just minutes before suddenly lifted. They exchanged looks of disbelief. The room was packed. Dozens of children held up homemade signs that asked for a school for Attawapiskat. Banners covered the walls. Shannen knew that other schools supported them, but actually seeing proof was overwhelming. As special guests, Shannen and her friends were escorted to the front. They stood in front of a sign that read, Enough of Your Greediness—Keep Your Promises!

Young men sat in a circle around a drum pounding a steady rhythm, while girls stood behind, fingers on their throats, supporting the drummers singing traditional songs with their

Shannen joined the crowd at the Peetabeck Academy in Fort Albany.

RIGHT: Tesla Koostachin and Sky Koostachin performed the Fancy Shawl dance.

high-pitched voices. Shannen's heart pulsed in perfect time with the beats and the music grabbed hold of her spirit. Katrina's family performed traditional dances in stunning regalia—the girls did the Fancy Shawl dance and her brother performed a Grass dance. The healing sounds of the tin cones on the Jingle dresses, tinkling like falling rain, flooded her with a feeling of comfort

and well-being. When it came time to read her speech, Shannen felt a powerful connection, an overwhelming sense of belonging in the presence of her people. Instead of being nervous, she felt the Seven Grandfathers giving her the strength to speak with Truth, Bravery, Wisdom, Respect, Humility, Honesty, and Love.

After, children held Sacred Fire candles. The day of drumming, dancing, and prayers ended with a powerful plea from the band leaders, "We need to come together as a People and build our spiritual strength to fight for more funding for First Nations education," one of them said. As she left the rally, Shannen was pumped with confidence and determination to see this fight to the end—to get a new school for the children of Attawapiskat.

Tara Stephen, Ashley Sutherland, Chris Kataquapit, and Shannen Koostachin spoke at the Sacred Fire Rally in Fort Albany.

Back home that evening before bed, Shannen told her sister all about Peetabeck Academy. "Oh, Serena, it was so awesome," Shannen said. "But it was also depressing. Their students are getting a much better education."

"I know," said Serena. "ShanShann...I don't want you to get upset, but...that's why I've decided to go a high school in the south for grade eleven."

"You want to move away from home?" Shannen cried, all of a sudden feeling the strength within her fall away.

"Shhh! Not so loud," whispered Serena. "I don't want to leave, but Vezina won't prepare me for university."

"Do Mama and Papa know?" Shannen asked.

"I've been talking with them, and to Mooshoom, too," Serena said. "They don't want me to leave, but they also want me to have the best education possible. Grandfather thinks that I will have better opportunities to learn more about our culture."

As much as it pained her to think of her sister living far away, Shannen could understand what Serena was saying. The Sacred Fire Ceremony had left her with an aching to learn more about being Cree—to dance at Powwows, to sing traditional songs, and to learn more history. However, the thought of Serena leaving home gave Shannen a different kind of ache, as if a fist had bruised the center of her chest.

"I've heard there is an excellent high school in New Liskeard," said Serena.

Shannen buried her face in her pillow. She couldn't imagine Attawapiskat without her sister. However, it was also true that most of the students who go to Vezina drop out and have problems coping with life on the reserve. She didn't want Serena to be one of those kids. And she was beginning to think a tough decision lay ahead for her, too.

The next evening after the younger kids were in bed, Serena sat on the chair beside the couch where her parents were watching television with Shannen and Julius. Shannen snuggled closely to her mother while her sister told them about her plans to go to high school in New Liskeard.

"We will have to find a good family for you to stay with," said her father, trying to hide his sadness.

After church on Sunday, Shannen's great-grandmother said nothing about Serena's decision, but Shannen could tell that she was unhappy. "It's not like residential school, Jaban," Shannen said to reassure her. "Serena wants to be there, and she will have many more opportunities."

Jaban did not look convinced.

CHAPTER 10
The Right Thing to Do

"I don't want others to go to school in portables that leak, windows don't open, washroom doors don't close, and ceilings are cracked. This is not an atmosphere for learning."

Shannen Koostachin, 13, 2008

The only thing keeping Shannen's mind off Serena's decision was the buzz from the Sacred Fire rally. If she'd had any doubts before, after seeing Peetabeck Academy and experiencing the spiritual strength of her people now she truly believed that anything was possible.

On Monday, Shannen spoke to her class. "At the rally, everyone was talking about the National Aboriginal Day of Action at the end of May. Hundreds of people will come to Ottawa to protest poverty on reserves." Shannen's eyes sparkled at the thought of her people standing up and speaking out for their rights. "The National Chief will talk about our campaign, so the whole country will know about Attawapiskat!"

Jonah cleared his throat, indicating that he had something to say. Shannen was in such a good mood, she hoped he wasn't going to spoil it by saying something negative.

"Yes, Jonah?" Carinna asked.

Everyone waited patiently while Jonah hesitated. "Um…" Jonah paused, and looked down.

Finally, he blurted, "Instead of going to Niagara Falls and Toronto in May, maybe we should go to Ottawa. We should go and talk to the minister ourselves." Then he blushed and looked down again.

The room fell silent. Not even Shannen could say a word. She didn't breathe for what seemed like minutes.

Brendon chuckled. "Good one!" Other kids broke out laughing, too. Shannen studied Jonah's expression for clues.

He's serious, she decided. Jonah was suggesting they go to Ottawa!

Shannen's heart was beating like hummingbird wings. There's no way the class will go for this, she thought. They had worked hard all year to raise money and now the students were counting the days. Even so, she bravely took the plunge. "Jonah, that's a great idea! Serena loved Ottawa." The image of Serena shaking the minister's hand flashed across her mind. "She met important people."

"And look how that turned out," scoffed Brendon.

Shannen was tempted to say something just as snarky, but she wanted to know what the others thought first. Instead she said, "Maybe we can convince this minister to change his mind, too."

Then Chris started to speak, slowly. "I think..."

Shannen knew that, like Jonah, he was taking time to think carefully about what to say, but the wait was agonizing.

"I was really looking forward to going to Niagara Falls. I've wanted to go there my whole life." Chris paused while the kids nodded and mumbled their agreement. Shannen's heart sank. "But, as soon as Jonah suggested going to Ottawa, I knew in my heart that it is the right thing to do."

Shannen fought the urge to smother her friend in a big bear hug. If Chris was for it, she was sure others would follow suit. Playing it cool, she told them more about the Day of Action.

Solomon was intrigued by the idea of such a large protest. "We can bring our signs," he said.

"And yell," Ashley broke into their chant. "We want a new school!"

Shannen added, "My sister said that when she was in Ottawa protesters beat drums and chanted while they marched. They wore regalia, too."

"But what about our grad dresses?" asked Stephanie, shyly.

"Ottawa has great shopping areas since it's a tourist desti-nation," said Carinna. Then she offered another suggestion. "Camp Wenonah is on the way. We could spend a couple of days there, then carry on to Ottawa for two days of shopping. After the rally, I think we could still visit Toronto and stop by Canada's Wonderland on the way home."

Shannen silently thanked Carinna. She could hardly sit still as she waited to hear what the rest of the class was thinking.

"I say let's go for it," said Chris.

Brendon listened for his friends' responses, then shrugged his shoulders. "What the heck. If you guys want to go, I'll go, too."

One by one, all the students came around to the idea. Shannen thought her heart would burst. Carinna looked happy, too. "We'll have to discuss this at the trip meeting tomorrow to get the approval of your parents and the school board."

Shannen beamed, thinking to herself, "No problem."

Things had been a bit subdued in the Koostachin household since Serena broke the news about leaving home. But on Monday evening, Shannen's father burst into the house with a grin on his face. "I got a phone call from a friend of ours who is offering to take in Serena next year."

"Who? Who? Who?" Shannen and Serena asked, excitedly.

Laughing, their father put his hand to his ear. "Do I hear owls?"

"Which friend?" they hollered, impatiently.

"Charlie Angus."

The sisters looked at each other with their eyes wide open in surprise, looking very much like owls indeed.

The next day, Emma announced sheepishly, "My parents don't want us to go to Ottawa."

It was like the wind had knocked Shannen off her feet. "Why?" she cried.

Shannen soon learned that other parents were not happy, either. "This doesn't mean we have to give up," Shannen said, hiding her own fears. "My father says that if you believe in something, stand up and speak for what you believe."

Jonah agreed. "We need to stick together and convince our parents that we really need to go to Ottawa."

"We can do it!" Shannen said, with all the confidence she could muster. "We just need to keep walking in our moccasins."

Later, at the trip meeting, one parent said, "Politics is for adults, not kids."

"You're right!" said another. "I don't want my kid sacrificing his trip to Niagara Falls for nothing. The government isn't going to change. It's just a waste of time."

Other parents mumbled in agreement.

Carinna had bad news as well. "The School Board is also worried that the students will be hurt and disappointed."

Then Shannen's father spoke. "I don't want that either, but these kids are afraid that their community will not get their school. Doing nothing does not overcome fear. Only action will overcome fear."

Then Chris jumped in, "We have our whole life to visit Niagara Falls."

Jonah added, "Even though we want to go to Niagara Falls, we want a school for Attawapiskat more."

The other students nodded.

The principal stood up and smiled proudly at her students. "I believe this is a good opportunity. It is their graduation trip, after all. If this is want they truly want, let's give them our blessing."

Much to Shannen's relief, murmurs of approval spread through the room.

CHAPTER 11
Any Volunteers?

"Kids in portables, it's not ideal, but it's not unheard of either. My own children spent a lot of time in portables."

Minister of Indian Affairs and Northern Development, 2008

"I guess you miss your tropical island, eh Carinna?" Shannen said to her teacher, who was flat on her back at the bottom of the icy portable steps.

"Very funny," said Carinna, looking up into the faces of several concerned students. "This is the second time I've fallen today."

"Hey, you wiped out real good!" said Chris, helping Carinna to her feet. "Are you hurt?"

"Just my pride," Carinna said, adding, "I can't wait to see what Attawapiskat looks like underneath all the snow when it finally melts."

77

Shannen lifted her eyebrows. "You mean, what Attawapiskat looks like underneath all that water. Didn't anyone tell you about the spring floods?" A look of worry spread across Carinna's face, as Shannen pressed on. "When the snow melts and the ice on the river breaks up, sometimes there are floods. If that happens, we get evacuated. We call it our spring vacation down south."

Shannen loved poking fun at the new teachers. Most of them were not as good sports about it as Carinna. Some were downright racist. A lot of them just couldn't see past the problems of

The Koostachin family often went camping. From left, Bryan Wabie, Serena, Andrew, Mickiso, Jenny, Raven, and Shannen.

living on the rez. Shannen knew that reserve life could sometimes be difficult, but she couldn't imagine living anywhere else.

"There's going to be a press conference the day before the Day of Action rally," Shannen said, as they walked towards the gym at the recreation center.

"Media attention is very important," Carinna replied.

"Serena told me that after her press conference, the whole country knew about the school campaign."

"Has anyone volunteered to speak?"

"Chris wants to. We asked Jonah because if he hadn't made the suggestion we wouldn't be going to Ottawa at all. But Jonah's very shy with strangers. Solomon offered because he gave a speech in his old community." Shannen had volunteered, too, of course. "We're going to write a letter to ask to speak with the INAC (Indian and Northern Affairs Canada) minister, but Charlie doesn't think he'll agree to meet us."

Shannen drifted into a recurring fantasy where she stands tall and proud in front of the minister, dressed in the beautiful blue regalia she hopes to have one day. She explains the teachings of the Seven Grandfathers, especially the importance of humility and respect. She describes how the children feel about being ignored and treated worse than other Canadian children. "Kindness is very important to our people." At this point, a big tear rolls down the minister's cheek. "I don't want my precious brothers and sisters to go to school in frigid, leaky, fire-traps. It's hard to feel pride when mice run over our food. It's hard to feel you can have the chance to grow up to be somebody important when you don't have proper resources, like a library." Now the minister is sobbing. "Stop! Stop!" he pleads. "Finally, I understand, Shannen. Thank you!" The fantasy always had the same ending—the minister shakes her hand to seal the promise—just like the other minister did with Serena.

"Shannen, are you listening?" Carinna asked. "I said just remember that you must be prepared for disappointment."

Shannen shrugged. "I know. My dad said the same thing."

"Hey, man! What's that sound?" Shannen whispered in a low and deep voice, searching the sky. Carinna looked up, too. A flock of honking geese flew by. Shannen sang out, "I hear foo-oo-ood."

After she finished laughing at her own joke, Shannen asked, "So, Carinna, are you going home for the Goose Break?"

The Cree say the sound of the geese on their way home to lay eggs is a call to return to their roots. In Attawapiskat, this sound also signals the start of the traditional Spring Goose Hunt. Every year for two weeks Attawapiskat becomes a ghost town as entire families, from great-grandparents to newborns, head out to their family camps on large wooden sleds hitched to snowmobiles to *nitao*—hunt, trap, and fish.

The Goose Hunt is an important time for elders to teach their children about Cree culture and rituals. The men instruct boys about the safe way to handle firearms and tend fires. "A fire is like a child. You have to watch it so it won't run away," Mooshoom told them. They learn how to set up blinds, make mud decoys, and imitate the honking of the geese. The women teach the girls where to find berries, how to trap small animals in the bush, and to prepare the geese for smoking.

Akimiski Island, in James Bay, is where Shannen's family camped.

Shannen's family camped on Akimiski Island, in James Bay. Everyone had a job to do. While the men hunted, the girls checked their grandmother's traps see if there was a rabbit or squirrel to bring back, and collected kindling for the campfires. The women prepared a Feast of barbecued goose and bannock. After a long day, the family sat around the fire with hot cups of tea bloss, eating s'mores, laughing at jokes and telling ghost stories. If they were lucky, the colorful *Wawahtay*—Northern Lights—would swirl across the sky. "Spirits of children past are dancing," Kookum explained.

The elders told legends and sang songs that had been passed down for generations. "We are bush and water people—the land and the water are in our spirit. We have lived and hunted on this land since the glaciers melted five thousand years ago," Mooshoom said. The children fell asleep one by one to the familiar sounds of their elders' voices and the crackling of the fire.

This was an especially important Goose Hunt for the Koostachins. Next year Serena would not have the time off school. It would be the first time the whole family was not together. Shannen was doing her best to cherish every moment—even the plucking.

CHAPTER 12
A Great Place for a Powwow

"There are diamonds on the coast of James Bay that people move mountains to get at. . . . And down the road from that there are kids living in poverty without grade schools."

Charlie Angus, MP, Timmins James Bay, 2010

After the Goose Break, their father decided to take Serena to visit Charlie Angus for a weekend to discuss plans for the coming year. Shannen insisted on going along. She was still grappling with the idea of her sister leaving and she thought it might put her mind at rest to see where Serena would be living. (She was also more than a little curious to see Charlie's house!)

Charlie and his wife, Brit, and their daughter, Lola, greeted the Koostachins warmly. The house was not at all what the sisters expected. Instead of a new and modern city house, it was old, and had old-fashioned furnishings. It was also eerily quiet, and tidy. The second day, Charlie took them to visit Timiskaming

Secondary School. The first thing the girls noticed was the grass that covered not only the front lawns but a large sports field in the back. A great place for a Powwow, thought Shannen.

When Shannen and Serena entered through the school's front doors, Shannen was overcome by the same welcoming feeling as when she had visited Peetabeck Academy.

"I am definitely coming to school here!" she exclaimed loudly, without even thinking about the students behind the closed classroom doors.

Their father looked at Charlie uncomfortably. The possibility that Shannen might also leave home to go to high school had never been discussed—let alone where she would live if she did. The Angus family had offered to take in one house guest, not two.

But Shannen was oblivious to the thoughts racing through the others' minds. "If I come to live with Charlie too, you won't be so lonely, Serena," she went on excitedly. "We could both get a good education together."

Serena was shocked at her sister's boldness and said nothing. Their father opened his mouth to speak, but Charlie interrupted. "I would have to square this with my wife—that's if your parents give their permission, Shannen."

Shannen's smile stretched impossibly wide.

Over the next few weeks, Shannen was so busy getting ready for the trip to Ottawa that she didn't have time to dwell on the frightening prospect of leaving home to go to high school.

"I want my speech to be as good as possible, because this time the whole country will be listening," Shannen said to Serena, chewing the end of her pencil. Her mind was drawing a perfect blank. All she could think of was what Serena had said in Ottawa—"I think we are the forgotten children of Attawapiskat." And here we are three years later, coming back to remind the government of the same thing? Shannen's mind was racing. Then her eyes widened and she started scribbling quickly before her idea vanished.

Finally, the last week in May arrived and the grade eight kids and their chaperones climbed into the small plane to begin their journey. After they landed in Timmins, they boarded a bus that took them farther south to Camp Wenonah. Most of the kids were too excited to sleep during the ten-hour drive, even though they had risen early that morning and had had a restless sleep the night before. While the boys played video games, the girls compared shopping lists and showed each other pictures in magazines of prom dresses they liked.

Norbert Paulmartin, one of the chaperones—and Stephanie's uncle—handed Chris a container of soil from the school site. "I brought this for you to give to the minister."

Chris laughed. "I'd like to see the expression on the minister's face when he takes a whiff of that."

"Ugh!" said Shannen. "I'll ask him if he still thinks there are no health and safety concerns."

The long bus ride gave Shannen lots of time to get even more nervous about the press conference. She tried to read magazines, but wasn't taking anything in. Different scenarios kept playing over and over in her head. At one point, she stuck out her hand to Ashley, saying, "I need to practice shaking hands. I don't want important people to think I'm just a dumb, little kid."

"But you are a dumb, little kid," Jonah said from the seat behind. Shannen leaped up from her seat and whacked him with her magazine.

The bus arrived at Camp Wenonah just as the sun painted the sky with broad brushstrokes of red and orange. As they piled out of the stale bus, they were met with fresh Muskoka air, infused with the scent of the majestic white pines that towered around them—so different from the scrawny, stunted trees back home. The kids were twitching to climb the massive outcropping of pink and gray Canadian Shield granite that flanked the parking lot on one side—in Attawapiskat it was hard to find a rock big enough to sit on.

"Oh, Carinna you were so right," breathed Shannen. "I've never seen a more beautiful place."

The students spent the next two days canoeing, kayaking, and rock climbing. Shannen was having such a great time, she

The grade eight grads posed for a photo at Camp Wenonah.

TOP: Shannen climbing at Camp Wenonah
BOTTOM: Mike Kataquapit and the grade eight students canoeing

hardly even thought about the campaign. It wasn't until she was back on the bus headed to Ottawa that the butterflies started their annoying fluttering in her stomach.

The bus moved like a giant metal snail through the crowded downtown streets of Ottawa, on the way to the university residences where the group would be staying. Kids jostled for window space, overwhelmed by the vast number of people and the towering buildings all jammed together. In Attawapiskat, Shannen always had a clear view of the horizon far in the distance. Here, even the sky seemed crowded.

"It's always slow during rush hour," the bus driver tried to explain over the noise of his impatient passengers.

"Hey, man, look at that," said Shannen, pointing to a woman draped in a black robe with two kids in tow. Only the woman's eyes showed through her head covering.

At the same time, they passed a group of African men. Their brightly patterned tunics jumped out against the steady flow of gray suits walking by. "Toto, we're not in Atta anymore," Jonah said, pretending to scratch behind Shannen's ear like she was a dog.

When they saw an Aboriginal street person panhandling

for change, Shannen and Ashley exchanged uncomfortable glances. Many Aboriginal people left their homes for a better life in the city, only to find disappointment. I wonder if he's from Attawapiskat, Shannen asked herself, sadly.

"Here we are, folks," called the driver.

"I'm starving," said Solomon, on the way to the university dormitory. A lot of the students were itching to find the malls and their food courts, but Shannen was in a trance. University was something Shannen had imagined many times. But the real thing was so much more impressive. She often talked with Ocean and Katrina about what they wanted to do when they were older. Shannen knew one thing for sure—she wanted to go to a university just like this.

Their rooms were bright and shining clean. Shannen breathed in the freshness of a pillow, losing herself in a daydream.

"Hey, sister!" Ashley yelled, whacking her awake with a pillow. "We have some serious shopping to do."

Shannen came out of her daydream swinging. "You asked for it," she said, laughing.

CHAPTER 13
The Children Have a Voice

"I want the minister to know that we will not wait for another eight years. He knows that we are sick and tired of walking outside in the cold. He knows these things. It's just that he doesn't understand."

Shannen Koostachin, 13, 2008

At breakfast the next morning, while the other students were shopping, Shannen, Solomon, and Chris practiced their speeches. Several elders and leaders from Attawapiskat had also arrived at the university, including Shannen's parents and her grandfather, John B. They had arranged to walk together to the House of Commons for the press conference.

As the group turned a corner and saw Parliament Hill for the first time, Shannen was overwhelmed by the sea of red and yellow. "Holay, tulips!" she exclaimed. She had never seen such beautiful flowerbeds and manicured lawns—or such majestic buildings. The gray and brown stone structures spanned the

Protesters at the Day of Action
on Parliament Hill, May 29, 2008

width of an entire city block. Shannen tried to disguise her feeling of awe. She was angry with the government, after all.

"I wouldn't want to change those batteries," said Chris, pointing up to the clock in the soaring Peace Tower.

John B. said, "Do you know that where we are standing, this home of the Canadian government, is built on unsurrendered Algonquin land?"

Solomon snorted. "Surprise, surprise!" But the mood was cheerful, and the kids broke out singing the popular Aboriginal version of the Canadian national anthem, "Oh, Canada! Your home's on Native land."

Chris Kataquapit, Shannen Koostachin, and Solomon Rae
pose with a rally poster at the Ottawa demonstrations.

Charlie Angus met the group at the large arched doors of the Center Block. Shannen admired his black suit. Charlie's formal appearance was unfamiliar, but his presence had a calming effect. "Omigawd, this is really happening," she squealed softly, as they passed through security on their way to the press gallery.

"Wow, this place is like a castle," whispered Solomon, his voice cracking against his will.

Chris agreed. "Ever old!"

The boys bumped into each other, gaping in every direction—up at the vaulted ceilings, down at the gleaming marble floors, around at the stone columns and leaded glass windows.

Solomon Rae, Charlie Angus, and Shannen Koostachin
wait for the press conference to begin.

The pressroom was dark and quiet as the group filed in and took their place by the podium, but it lit up suddenly with cameras flashing and bright glaring lights. Reporters took their places in the seats in front of a row of large TV cameras. Shannen's heart seemed to be hammering in her ears. She glanced sideways at the frozen expressions on the faces of Chris and Solomon.

Behind them were the flags of Canada's provinces and territories. Shannen gulped, only then feeling the full impact of what she was about to do. This was the whole country she was speaking to, not just a roomful of people like in Fort Albany. This was their chance to convince all Canadians to support their fight, to bring hope and change to their community. She was just glad she wasn't speaking first. She tried to breathe deeply and calm her nerves.

Chris was the one who spoke first, thanking the thousands of students who took the time to write letters and spread their messages. "The children have a voice!" Shannen was amazed at how cool and natural he sounded, even though his papers quivered in his hand. He talked about giving up Niagara Falls to come to Ottawa. "We have waited long enough. We want what every other student in Canada has—a good school."

As Shannen approached the microphone, her heart pounded like a drum. She took a deep breath.

"Three years ago, my sister, Serena Koostachin, here on this same spot, pleaded for a new school for our community. She sat in on a meeting where the minister promised us a school." Shannen felt a surge of anger as she spoke the word "promised." Her voice got stronger, as she emphasized each word. "But, I ask, why do I have to come back and do the same thing once again? As young people, we are told to keep our promises. But our own government cannot keep a promise that they have made three times."

Solomon was next. He stood tall, holding his chin high as he spoke. "I am here on behalf of my younger sisters and brothers who don't know what a real school looks like. I am here on behalf of the kindergarten students who have to walk ten minutes just to go to gym class in minus forty-degree weather. I am here on behalf of our disabled students who have to wheel their wheelchairs through snow and ice. I am here on behalf of the students who have already dropped out because they have no hope. I am here on behalf of a community that has been let down one too many times." Shannen was amazed that Solomon could speak with such power—and from memory. Solomon addressed his last words directly to the minister. "You have the power to give us a school. Meegwetch."

The three friends congratulated each other with their eyes.

From the press conference, the group was taken to another room where a luncheon for the Attawapiskat visitors was being held. There they met up with the rest of their grade eight class. There were also teachers and students there who had traveled from St. Edmund Campion Secondary School in Brampton, near Toronto. The students swarmed the Attawapiskat kids, excited to meet their heroes.

"I feel like a rock star," Brendon whispered to Shannen, wearing a silly grin.

One of the girls overheard and asked shyly, "Are you Shannen, the one who made the video?" She eagerly called her classmates over when Shannen nodded.

The students told them about their "Attawapishack."

"It's a booth we made for our school atrium. We collected protest letters and raised awareness about reserve schools." Attawapishack—that was funny, but they had no idea what an atrium was.

One of the teachers handed Jonah a box filled with messages of hope for each of the four hundred students at J.R. "We also gave Charlie Angus two thousand letters to present to the minister."

"Cool t-shirts," said Solomon.

Solomon Rae was proud to wear a t-shirt from the students of St. Edmund Campion Secondary School in Brampton, Ontario.

A boy with dreads said, "We designed them."

On the front of the white shirt was written, "A school for the children of Attawapiskat." He turned so they could read the back. "Never doubt that a small, thoughtful group of committed citizens can change the world. Indeed, it is the only thing that ever has." Underneath was a name—Margaret Mead.

One of the kids explained, "The most successful changes in history are 'grassroots'—from people's actions from the ground up rather than from the top down."

They offered shirts to the Attawapiskat kids. "Cool," said Brendon. "I'll wear it at the rally tomorrow."

While the guests munched on little sandwiches and raw vegetables, politicians and Aboriginal leaders made speeches— including the National Chief, who fondly remembered his visit to Attawapiskat. Charlie ended with exciting news, "The minister has agreed to meet with some students," he said, eyes flashing. "This is a very good sign!"

Shannen clasped her hands to her open mouth. This was her

chance to make her dream a reality! She bounced on her toes. "Can I go to the meeting?" she asked.

"What about the same three students who were at the press conference?" Charlie asked.

Solomon shook his head. "I think Jonah should be there. It was his idea to come to Ottawa in the first place."

Jonah looked at the floor, still holding the box of cards and letters. Shannen put her arm around his shoulder. "Jonah, you must seize this opportunity! You can do it!" Then she added, "Don't be scared. Chris and I will be right there with you."

Jonah nodded his head slightly.

When the luncheon was over, John B. asked everyone to hold hands in a circle. While he said a prayer, Shannen felt the Seven Grandfathers supporting her again, especially the Grandfather of Love. She closed her eyes and thought, Nothing is stronger than love.

Northern students lobby for long-promised school

BY ARIELLE GODBOUT

After eight years of waiting for a new school, students from Attawapiskat in northern Ontario have had enough.

The group of 21 Grade 8 students cancelled their graduation trip to Niagara Falls and came to Ottawa to protest instead.

They held a news conference on Parliament Hill yesterday morning to describe the condition of the portables they use for classrooms — windows and doors that don't always close, ceilings that leak and washrooms with very little privacy.

"They're just all scattered buildings and we always have to walk 10 minutes just to go to gym," said student Shannen Koostachin. "I got sick twice from coming out of the gym all sweaty and cold."

She said it's also embarrassing and disruptive because the washrooms are in the same portable as the classroom.

"We ... are the generation of students who have never seen a real school," Chris Kataquapit said. "That is why we made the decision to come to Ottawa."

Attawapiskat is an isolated reserve near James Bay that is only accessible by plane. The community's school was closed in 2000 after students and teachers became sick due to contamination from a diesel spill, said Charlie Angus, MP for Timmins-James Bay.

The Department of Indian and Northern Affairs promised a new school at the time, but the students have been waiting ever since, he said.

"Indian Affairs gets away with this kind of thing because it's out of sight, out of mind," Mr. Angus said.

Assembly of First Nations National Chief Phil Fontaine, who met with students later in the day, said Attawapiskat is just one of 40 aboriginal communities across Canada that is lacking adequate school facilities.

"We ask ourselves if the response from government would have been different if this was a situation in Toronto, Ottawa, (or) any urban community in the country," Chief Fontaine said.

He has invited the students to join him today for the national day of action in support of First Nations.

CHAPTER 14
We Are Not Going Away

"Shannen knew that she was speaking up not only for her community, but for lots of other Aboriginal kids across Canada who don't have equity in education."

Stan Louttit, Grand Chief, Mushkegowuk Council, 2008

The next day, the group from Attawapiskat who would be attending the meeting with the minister met at the entrance to the House of Commons. Shannen was comforted by the presence of Annabella Iahtail, a revered *Okimaw*, or teacher, who had taught generations of children the language, culture, and values of their Cree ancestors at the school. John B. and Shannen's parents came along for support. Shannen leaned against her father. "My stomach feels funny," she said, wishing her parents could be with her at the meeting.

"I'm sure it's just nerves," said her mother, noticing that Chris and Jonah looked pale, too.

While they waited for Charlie Angus, Shannen's father gave advice to the students. "Remember to be polite, no matter what the minister says. Treat him just as you would your own elders—with respect." Shannen rolled her eyes, thinking, But my elders deserve respect.

Charlie's assistant arrived carrying black t-shirts made for the Aboriginal Day of Action.

"Cool!" said Chris.

Shannen tugged the shirt over her head, struggling to get her thick ponytail through the neck opening. "How do I look?" she asked, loose strands of hair flying about her face.

"Still ugly," said Chris, quickly adding, "Just joking, einh-einh!"

Shannen and the group gathered on the steps of the House of Commons before their meeting with the minister.

"Where's Charlie?" Shannen asked. His assistant looked flustered, as she kept checking her phone for messages. "He's trying to find out the location of the meeting. They keep changing it."

Shannen didn't think that sounded like a good sign.

Once the location of the meeting had been fixed, Charlie's assistant led the group into the building. Shannen's knees felt wobbly. She clung to her mother for support as they walked through the hallways. When they arrived at the door, Shannen was struck with a startling thought.

"I wish I had my speech!" she said, suddenly seized with panic.

"Just speak from your heart, danis," her father said. If only her heart would stop pounding!

"We'll be right here," her mother whispered.

A cheerful aide greeted the group, then ushered them through an office into a huge meeting room. Shannen felt like Alice in Wonderland after drinking from the bottle that made her small. As she gaped at the rich marble fireplace, the high, ornate wood ceiling and the large tapestries that hung on each wall, she reached out for the security of Annabella's arm. This beloved elder with her long, steel-gray hair seemed just as small and out of place in the grand room.

Several men and women in suits sat in armchairs around a

long glass-topped table. The students recognized the minister as soon as he stood up. "Ever big," whispered Jonah. Shannen poked him with her sharp elbow.

The minister towered over them as he smiled down at the students, extending his hand. When Shannen offered her hand in return, she felt as if she was placing a delicate bird in a catcher's mitt, but his grip was surprisingly gentle.

"I understand that you've come a long way to speak with me," he said, startling her with his booming voice. "How do you like this room?"

Without missing a beat, Shannen shot back, "This room is

This is the meeting room where the group met the minister.

bigger than our whole portable. I wish we had a classroom as nice as this office. Kids would be there every day."

Jonah's jaw dropped to the floor. Chris's eyebrows hit the ceiling. They didn't dare catch each other's eye for fear of cracking up.

Shannen's bold move gave them courage.

"Now," the minister said, getting down to business, "I understand that you young people want to talk to me about your school."

Chris stepped forward and handed over the jar of smelly soil. The minister thanked Chris and placed it, unopened, on his desk.

Then Jonah spoke. "Can you make us a promise—?"

The minister interrupted. "No, son, I'm afraid that I can't make any promises," he said, shaking his head.

It was so sudden. Jonah looked as if he had been slapped. Annabella gently placed her hand on his shoulder.

Shannen looked at her friend helplessly. What does he mean he can't make promises? Of course he can make promises! Shannen's cheeks flamed. Nothing seemed right. She felt like a train hurled off its tracks.

The Mushkegowuk Chief stepped forward, "Minister, the children want to know..."

Shannen could not listen. She backed her way to the door,

slowly, so no one would notice. She couldn't let them see her cry. Then Shannen slipped out of the office and into her mother's waiting arms.

"*Moonaneh, gawenah mateh*," her mother whispered. "Don't give up now, my daughter."

"Remember the Seven Grandfathers. One is Bravery, Shannen!" said her father. Then he gave his daughter something she found impossible to resist—his smile. She tried her best to offer a smile in return. Then she picked herself up and walked back into the meeting.

Chris and Jonah were so full of anger, that they had not even noticed Shannen leave. Chris looked about to scream. Instead, he swallowed and said, "We invite you to come to our community to understand our living situation." Shannen thought her father would be proud.

The minister shook his head again. "I'm afraid that's not possible, either. I have a very busy schedule. I do get reports from my staff, because I can't be everywhere at one time." The minister turned to the elders. "I admit that there is a lot to do in your community, I admit that, and I do not claim that it's all done. All these things are expensive. They've got to be done and we're working through a list of priorities." Then he addressed the students again. "These portables, I admit, are not ideal. The easy thing for me to do is to promise you a new school. But there are thirty to forty other schools that have more pressing needs." He sounded apologetic. "We simply do not have the money at this time."

Annabella spoke a few words in Cree. Shannen was relieved that everyone at the table was respectfully silent. Chief Hall translated her words. "Can you tell me when our children will get their new school?"

The minister replied, "To be honest, it will most likely be another fifteen years." Annabella pulled out a tissue and dabbed her eyes without looking up. Then, abruptly, the minister finished by saying, "Thank you for coming. I enjoyed meeting you all, but I am late for another meeting."

Shannen's eyes opened wide in shock. He was leaving? Just like that? The elders looked uncomfortable, but remained respectful as the minister shook each of their hands.

As the minister approached her, Shannen's face was as cold and hard as the granite she had just climbed two days before. When he offered his hand, she looked him straight in the eye. "We are not going away," she said. "The children are not going to quit. We are not going to give up until we have justice."

Chris and Jonah's lips quivered as if they might break into a fit of giggles. The elders looked surprised, too. Shannen had even surprised herself with her bold words, but it felt right to stand up and speak out for her beliefs and for her community.

CHAPTER 15
Seeds of Hope

"We ask ourselves if this response from government would be any different if this was the situation in Toronto, Ottawa, or any urban community in the country."

Phil Fontaine, National Chief, Assembly of First Nations, 2008

Shannen waited until the minister left, then she dissolved into tears. Angry tears. Hot, angry tears. She was angry with the minister. Angry with herself for failing to change his mind. Angry that her friends had sacrificed their trip to Niagara Falls for this. Her dream of helping her community had turned into a nightmare.

Her mother held her tight, stroking her hair.

"I wish I could just go home," Shannen sobbed.

"We're proud of you, danis. You should be proud, too. You did your best. Your best is all anyone can expect."

Shannen was not about to be comforted. Maybe her father

had been wrong. Maybe standing up and speaking out for what you believe in does not help. Maybe hope and prayers don't work, either. Maybe Jonah had been right all those weeks ago. The government doesn't care about us. Indians don't count for anything.

Jenny kept her arm around Shannen as they walked toward Victoria Island where the protest march was about to begin. By now, hundreds of people were gathered at the island. The drumming, and singing, and the bright rainbow colors of the regalia created a joyous and festive atmosphere, but the messages on the picket signs reminded everyone of the solemn occasion. Through her tears and anger, Shannen had to smile at a toddler chewing on a cardboard sign that said, "Education is a right."

"Hey, Shann, look at that awesome banner," said Jonah, gesturing the Cree way of pointing with his mouth at a banner that read, "Wouldn't it be cool if the kids from Attawapiskat had a school?"

Shannen walked toward her classmates. They carried the banners made by the high school art classes, decorated with blue handprints of kids from the nursery school. She could tell right away that they had been texted about the disappointing news. Annabella gathered the group together into a healing circle and spoke words of comfort in Cree. "My children, don't be sad. I know that you will get your school. It will just take longer, that is all."

Shannen's father, with Charlie at his side, stomped over to the Chief to find out exactly what was said in the meeting. "Why on Earth would the minister agree to a meeting with our children and then disappoint them?" her father fumed, shaking his head.

"This man has no honor," said the National Chief, not seeming to mind that his tears were evident.

"Maybe this was all a big mistake," said Charlie, rubbing his brow. "I feel responsible for this fiasco. Children should not have to face this kind of disappointment."

Amid all of this, Shannen was surprised to hear laughing. She turned her head to see Chris saying to Carinna, "You should have heard her."

Jonah interrupted, "Shannen said that she wished her class was as big as his office!"

Carinna's eyes bulged. Shannen suddenly wondered if she had said the wrong thing. "I hadn't planned to say those words— they just came out," she said to Carinna.

Carinna enveloped Shannen in a huge hug and began to laugh—loud, belly laughs. Chris and Jonah were clutching their sides, howling with laughter. "Then she said we were not going away," Chris barely managed to get out. "That we won't quit until there's justice."

Now the Mushkegowuk Chief was laughing too. He wiped his eyes with his sleeve and said, "I would never have had the courage to say those words when I was young, me!"

Shannen was confused. She was sad and crying and everyone else was laughing and crying. Are they nuts? she wondered. What's there to laugh at?

But laughter has a way of spreading, and Shannen caught the bug without knowing why. "You are all Cree-zy!" she managed to joke.

A crowd of reporters and photographers approached Shannen, Chris, and Jonah to ask about the meeting. "Do you really believe that the government has no money to build the school?"

"No, not one bit," Chris answered, confidently. "We believe that if the leaders could see the situation faced by the children on the James Bay coast they wouldn't be able to turn away from us and say that they have other 'priorities.'"

Shannen began to feel strength returning. "I don't think he should be saying our school is safe until he has walked in our moccasins," she added.

The reporters made notes when Jonah told them what Shannen said to the minister about his office. It began to occur to Shannen that although the meeting did not turn out as she had imagined, she was being given another chance to get their message out to the Canadian people. "I told the minister that the children were not giving up until we had justice," she said.

The delegation from Attawapiskat was asked to lead the march from Victoria Island to the Peace Tower they could see above the trees. Protesters carried signs, beat drums, and chanted, "Hey ya. Hey ya. Hey ya. Hey ya. Hey ya. Hey ya."

When they arrived at Parliament Hill, the students were given a position of honor at the top of the stairs with leaders and elders. A circle of drummers seated around the large ceremonial drum at the foot of the stairs performed a song ritual to open the Aboriginal Day of Action.

Shannen looked down at hundreds and hundreds of people gathered on the lawns below—elders and babies, university students, and teens in school uniforms. Girls in Jingle dresses and boys in feathered headdresses and regalia were practicing their dances. The familiar smell of sweetgrass wafting through the air calmed her. She filled with pride as she listened to First Nations leaders from across Canada speak about issues of justice and rights.

Just before the end of the protest, Charlie asked Shannen, "The emcee says we can squeeze in a student from Attawapiskat. Would you like to speak?" Shannen blinked like a startled young deer. "But I don't have my speech," she cried. Her eyes darted to her father.

"Just speak the truth," he whispered. "Find the words in your heart. Hi-ho mistahey!"

Prinz Sutherland, Michelle Kioke,
and Darren Taylor held the banner in Ottawa.

As Shannen's father led her to the microphone, she felt her shoulders tremble like butterfly wings. She began, "Today, I feel down because the minister said he didn't have the money to build our new school."

The crowd responded, "Shame! Shame!"

"I didn't believe it," Shannen continued. "It's not right. That is the reason why we are here today, to build this fight for a new school." She repeated what the minister said about other reserves having priority. "Maybe he thinks we will just lose hope

Ashley Sutherland, Marvin Kioke, and Chris Kataquapit, listen as Shannen speaks to crowd at the Days of Action.

and give up. But I was always taught by my parents to stand up and speak for what I believe in. I told him the children won't give up. We will keep moving forward, walking proud in our moccasins until we are given justice."

Standing in the crowd below, a woman listened to this passionate young girl with the long dark ponytail swaying in the breeze. She marveled at how someone so young could speak with such wisdom and strength about the injustices endured by her people. She made up her mind to speak to the girl.

The National Chief gave the last words of the day. He spoke about the despair felt by First Nations People, the despair of poverty and injustice in the past and in the present. "Decisions we make today to care and nurture our children," he said, "will be good for the seventh generation to come." He pointed to the student activists and his voice lifted. "Today I am full of hope for future generations because of the presence of these young people. By taking responsibility for those who follow in their footsteps, they have planted seeds of hope."

LEFT: The Day of Action march to Parliament Hill

CHAPTER 16
Three Little Words

"I believe in the power of youth. With every generation comes an opportunity to create a better world."

Cindy Blackstock, Executive Director, First Nations Child and Family Service Caring Society of Canada.

Canada's Wonderland was the perfect way to end their trip. You couldn't help but feel joyful after a trip to an amusement park. Shannen went on every ride possible. Her voice was hoarse from screaming, and her cheeks were sore from smiling about all their adventures on the bus ride back to Timmins.

"Remember when Norbert shook hands with the former Canadian prime minister? Mr. Paulmartin, meet Mr. Paul Martin." Everyone howled again as they watched Norbert try to squeeze the enormous stuffed animal he'd won at Canada's Wonderland through the door of the small cargo plane that took them home to Attawapiskat. Carinna topped it off by announcing trip joke awards over the inter-com. It was a trip to remember, that was for sure.

Shortly after the students were settled back into normal life, Shannen received a phone call. "I heard you speak in Ottawa," Cindy Blackstock said. "I'm honored to 'meet' you." Cindy went on to explain the reason for her call. "Have you heard

Carinna Pellett, the grad class teacher, loved to have fun. According to her, "You are never too old to wear a funny hat."

of the Convention on the Rights of the Child?" Shannen knew about First Nations treaty rights. She had not heard of this convention. Cindy said, "The United Nations wrote a special charter that guarantees rights to all children." Then she told the story of her young friend in grade five who had learned that a good education and a decent standard of living was a right according to that Convention. "When Clara saw your video, she cried. But, rather than just feeling sad, she took action. In a letter, her grade five class asked the Prime Minister why they had a decent school and children in Attawapiskat did not."

Shannen's eyebrows lifted. Did this mean that it was against the law to deny them a real school?

"A First Nations child is supposed to have the same education opportunities as other Canadians, yet the government provides less education funding for children on reserves. This racial discrimination limits your potential." Shannen thought back to what Charlie Angus had said about apartheid. "I want your young voices to be heard," Cindy said. "Would you and your friends write a letter to the United Nations Committee on the Rights of the Child about your fight for a new school?"

The silence stretched uncomfortably long while Shannen's thoughts moved from fear to intrigue and back to fear again. She recalled her father's words about action overcoming fear and seizing opportunities.

"I can ask the others," she said, her voice barely more than a whisper. "And my sister, too."

Shannen knew her friends might be hard to convince. They were still angry about the meeting with the minister. She felt

Article 3 of the Convention on the Rights of the Child

"The government shall ensure that the institutions, services and facilities responsible for the care or protection of children shall conform with the standards established by competent authorities, particularly in the areas of safety (and) health . . ."

the same way, but she knew an opportunity when one came knocking. The next day, Shannen approached Chris, Jonah, and Solomon.

"I don't know, Shannen," Chris said. "I suck at writing letters."

"But you write e-mails and texts all the time," said Shannen.

"Yeah." Solomon laughed. "But no adult could understand them."

"Serena will help us," said Shannen. "If we're going to be activists, we should learn how to write letters."

Jonah took his time before answering. He seemed to be mulling things over. "So we're snitching on the government…?"

"It sounds like fun when you put it that way," said Chris.

On June 11, 2008, Shannen sat in front of the large television screen with the residents of Attawapiskat who had come together in the community hall to watch the Canadian prime minister deliver an historic apology for the mistreatment of First Nations children who were taken from their parents and placed in schools off the reserves. There they were not allowed to speak their own languages and were often abused. "We now recognize that in separating children from their families, we undermined

'We are sorry'

Tears fall in hushed House of Commons as Prime Minister apologizes on behalf of nation for residential schools ordeal

BILL GRIMSHAW FOR THE TORONTO STAR

Assembly of First Nations national chief Phil Fontaine is hugged by his daughter Maya after Prime Minister Stephen Harper's apology yesterday.

LINDA DIEBEL
NATIONAL AFFAIRS WRITER

OTTAWA—Three little words: "We are sorry."

But these were history-making words yesterday, uttered in a hushed House of Commons by Prime Minister Stephen Harper to Canada's First Nations, Inuit and Métis peoples for their suffering in the once-obligatory residential school system.

As he spoke, school survivors wept in the public galleries, their tears a tribute to the tears of every mother who cried for a child forcibly taken from her over generations.

A man in the gallery held a lone eagle feather aloft for more than an hour, throughout the apology and subsequent speeches by opposition and aboriginal leaders.

The day began with the lighting of a sacred fire on an island in the Ottawa River in view of the Parliament Buildings where native peoples were legislated as "inferior" in 1874 and, in 1884, mandated by law to send their children away to residential schools.

It wound down after the apology with drumming and a ritual cleansing, the "smudging" ceremony in another part of the Centre Block.

"These are happy tears," said Holly Danyluk, a James Bay Cree.

The atmosphere among the many native families who had gathered on Parliament Hill was almost festive early in the afternoon, like a big family picnic. Old friends and family members reunited, pinched babies' cheeks and shared cold drinks and ice cream. Music played in the background in the form of traditional drumming and chanting.

But the crowd stilled and the mood turned solemn as the giant TV screen came to life and the

APOLOGY continued on A18

INSIDE

On the scene with the oldest and youngest survivors of the schools.
A17

Healing words and painful memories inside and outside the House of Commons.
A19

Star's view: Give Harper credit for his apology. Now he must act.
AA10

Text of the PM's apology, plus James Travers on the politics of indifference.
AA11

the ability of many to adequately parent their own children and sowed the seeds for generations to follow."

If the government was really sorry, they'd help us now, Shannen thought to herself, bitterly. Her stomach lurched as the camera paused on the face of the Indian Affairs Minister who, only ten days ago, had told them that they weren't a priority.

"The infamous goal of the residential schools was 'to kill the Indian in the child.' Today, we recognize that this policy of

Boys and girls at St. Anne's Residential School were separated, slept in dormitories, and ate their meals cafeteria-style.

assimilation was wrong, has caused great harm, and has no place in our country."

It hurt Shannen to see pain in the eyes of elders in the room—some of whom were reliving the horror of being plucked from their families. Parents who never laid eyes on their children after they were taken away, were still grieving their loss. Many died from illness. Two boys who ran away from St. Anne's, in Fort Albany, perished on their way back to see their mothers in Attawapiskat.

Did You Know?

- There are more than one million First Nations People in 615 communities in Canada. Aboriginal People are the youngest and fastest growing segment of Canada's population. One half the Aboriginal population is under 25.
- A First Nations child receives between $2,000 to $4,000 less funding for his/her education than a child in a provincial school.
- Health concerns in First Nations schools include: overcrowding, extreme mould, high carbon dioxide levels, sewage fumes in school, frozen pipes, unheated portables, students suffering from cold and frost bite, and schools being abandoned despite a lack of alternative infrastructure.
- Approximately 60 new schools are needed in First Nations communities nationally, and an additional 30 schools are in need of expansion and major renovations. There are 60 reserves with no schools.

Then Shannen recognized the National Chief, in full Ojibwe regalia and headdress, emotionally responding to the apology. "The memories of residential schools sometimes cut like a knife at our souls." He paused to regain his composure. "This day will help us to put that pain behind us."

Shannen remained surprisingly unmoved. All the research they had done for their letter to the UN led her to believe that they had not come all that far from the old residential school days. She knew that there were currently more Aboriginal children in

- One in four First Nations youth graduates from high school, half the rate of other Canadian youth.
- Canada's indigenous languages are among the most endangered in the world.
- One in four First Nations children lives in poverty, compared to one in nine in other Canadian children
- Twenty times the number of Aboriginal children are in government care than in the regular population.
- The rate of disabilities among First Nations children (about one in eight) is almost double the rate among Canadian children.
- More than one third of First Nations households with children are overcrowded.
- More than half of First Nations children are either overweight or obese.
- Suicide accounts for 38% of all deaths for First Nations youth aged 10-19.

government-sponsored foster care than there were at the height of the residential school system, because the government did not always make available to parents the basic things they needed to care for their kids—things like proper housing, clean water, and food. Shannen didn't fully understand why reserves were so poor if their ancestors had signed treaties to share in the wealth of Canada's natural resources, like the diamonds being mined near Attawapiskat.

What she was learning made her furious sometimes, depressed other times. But each time she and her friends uncovered another statistic about First Nations inequality and injustice, Shannen felt less afraid about writing the letter. When she had difficulty understanding the issues or felt unsure of herself, Cindy was always there to help explain things and reassure her. "An Aboriginal elder once told me that leaders accomplish great things when they have knowledge, passion, and spirit," she said. "Shannen, you already have all of these in abundance and you have put them to action."

Shannen thought back to the time when the grade eight class believed that they didn't have any power. Now they were writing a letter to the United Nations about their rights as children. Imagine that! More than ever, Shannen had faith in her beliefs. More than ever, she knew that taking action was right. It was possible for children to create a better world.

CHAPTER 17

Stepping Stones

"I would like people to know three things about me: One, I do not like broken promises. Two, I do not like seeing my siblings going to school in portables. And three, I would like them to know too that I AM NOT GIVING UP."

Shannen Koostachin, 13, 2008

Graduation from elementary school was a big deal in Attawapiskat, since not all kids on the reserve made it to grade eight. Families were overjoyed with their children's success. For most students, this would be their only graduation, since the secondary school dropout rate was high. To reward their accomplishment and make the students feel proud, the community went to a lot of effort to make the occasion memorable. Students from every grade made the decorations in the sportsplex gymnasium in the theme colors chosen by the graduating class. Each grad student had his or her photo framed in a Medicine Wheel. Mothers were insanely happy to see their sons looking so handsome in their suits. Boys squirmed as combs were forced through their hair before the first of many photos were taken. After the ceremony, everyone celebrated with a Feast.

Shannen wiggled into her sparkly new dress and tottered on high-heeled shoes. "Our little girl looks so grown up," her parents cried, making Shannen feel even more self-conscious. She was relieved when it was time to slip the white satin gown over her dress and put on the mortarboard hat worn by so many other grads over the years. She thought she looked dumb, but at least everybody else in the class did too.

Carinna teased the kids about their fancy clothes—payback for all the times they had laughed at her when she wore a dress. She had her camera ready to take pictures when the robes came off. To her chagrin, the students immediately put on their hooded sweatshirts. Carinna couldn't believe it! "Take those old things off," she yelled.

"You can't boss us anymore, Carinna," said Brendon, and they all laughed.

The growing success of the Students-Helping-Students campaign gave the 2008 graduating class even more reason to celebrate. To Shannen it felt like the campaign was a snowball, growing larger and faster as it rolled downhill. Thousands of people had watched the video. More than 100 schools had joined and other groups were hopping on board—and she knew the numbers would only grow in the next school term. It had been an amazing year, but Shannen was looking forward to a quiet and peaceful summer.

She also wanted to earn some cash for the money and school supplies she would need in the fall, not to mention that her new school had a mall nearby—her friends were probably more jealous about that than about the school! Shannen felt lucky to get part-time work at the band office and a convenience store.

On July 12th, Shannen celebrated her fourteenth birthday with many friends and her family picnicking at Akimiski Island. While the elders prepared the Feast—moose head roasted over the fire, hotdogs, marshmallows, and bannock, of course— Shannen walked with her friends along on the pebble beach where she chose pretty stones for her collection. They sat among the forget-me-nots near the lake talking and laughing—mostly laughing.

That day was an up day for Shannen. Other days were down. The reality of leaving home in the fall was hitting her for real now. So many different feelings were swirling inside. She worried about missing her family—their movie nights, snuggling together on a mattress in front of the TV, eating her father's famous nachos; tickling Dallas with butterfly kisses; reading stories to Codee, and walking her dog. She couldn't imagine Julius not being around to make her laugh so hard she would fall over sideways. She would even miss having Raven and Mickiso around to bug her when she wanted some peace and quiet. She worried about what kind of food there would be at Charlie's. How could it ever be as good as her mother's cooking? Would her grandparents and Jaban worry about them being so far away?

As if Shannen didn't have enough to think about, life became even more complicated with another phone call from Cindy Blackstock. Cindy read a newspaper article about their letter to the UN. "Attawapiskat students take battle to UN," it began. "A group of children from Attawapiskat are taking the fight for a school to the United Nations..."

"Shannen," Cindy said after she had read her the whole article, "I would like your permission to nominate you for a special honor."

It wasn't normal for Shannen to be speechless but she couldn't get her reply off her tongue. She just let Cindy continue.

"Every year a prize is awarded to a child who has devoted a lot of his or her energy to improve the rights of other children. It's called the International Children's Peace Prize." Shannen had heard about the peace prize that Nelson Mandela and Mother Teresa had won. But she had never heard of one for children. "All I need you to do is write a letter to the nomination committee about your fight to get a school built in your community. I will ask other people to write letters of recommendation, too. The winner gets to travel to Holland and receives a donation of one hundred thousand euros—that's about a hundred and fifty thousand dollars."

Shannen all of a sudden felt as if she was at the top of the biggest rollercoaster in Canada's Wonderland. Europe! Money! She felt like screaming for joy. Was this for real? Then Shannen's thrill level dropped just as suddenly. "But what about Chris, Jonah, and Solomon? They've worked just as hard. Our whole community worked together."

"Shannen, you're right. I want to nominate all the kids involved, but the rules of the Peace Prize won't allow it. I'm sure the others will understand. I'm sure they'll be happy for you."

Cindy gave Shannen some time to think.

"So what do you say? Do you want to write the letter?"

"I guess so," was all Shannen could muster.

When Serena heard about Cindy's call, she was over the moon. Shannen told her about her worries. "I wouldn't blame the other kids if they're mad at me!"

"I know how you feel, Shann. When I went to Ottawa, I didn't expect to be singled out either. I just wanted to speak for my community, like you did in Ottawa." Sometimes the sisters fantasized about being celebrities. Now Shannen was getting her first inkling that fame might be more complicated than she had envisioned.

"This is the most awesome news ever!" cried Katrina, hugging Shannen, who was still panting from her run over to her cousin's house. The girls rushed over to Katrina's mother's computer to look up the KidsRights website.

"I don't think I'll win. There will be lots of other kids nominated."

Shannen was curious to know what kind of actions other kids were nominated for. She found out that one winner helped child slaves in India. Another fought for the rights of children in Africa with HIV/AIDS. Most of the activists were from very poor countries. Shannen was surprised but deeply honored to be included in the same group with these children from all over the world.

"Hey! The girl who won last year led a fight for a school, too," Katrina said. "See, ShanShann. You have a good chance."

Shannen had written so many speeches by now, she didn't think it would be hard to write a letter. But it was different writing about herself. It made her feel uncomfortable to answer questions about her personality and leadership skills. She didn't want to be stuck-up. When she couldn't think of what to write, she'd drift off and imagine what it would be like to win the prize. Shannen knew better than to get her hopes up, but it was hard not to be swept away. She thought of what her grandmother would say. "Don't go counting your chickens before they're hatched!" It was Shannen's idea to write the letter in both English and Cree. She wanted to make her kookum proud.

After Cindy sent the nomination off to the committee, she arranged another press conference to make the announcement. Shannen listened to Cindy from the Wawatay news radio station in the band office so the media could phone her after for interviews.

"This is how one girl from one northern community, with the company of other children, says 'I'm going to change the world'—and she did. Shannen has demonstrated leadership, courage, and generosity in her school and community. Thousands have answered her call to action. The inspiring and determined action taken by Shannen and her fellow student ambassadors have made the Attawapiskat School Campaign the largest child-led children's rights movement in Canadian history."

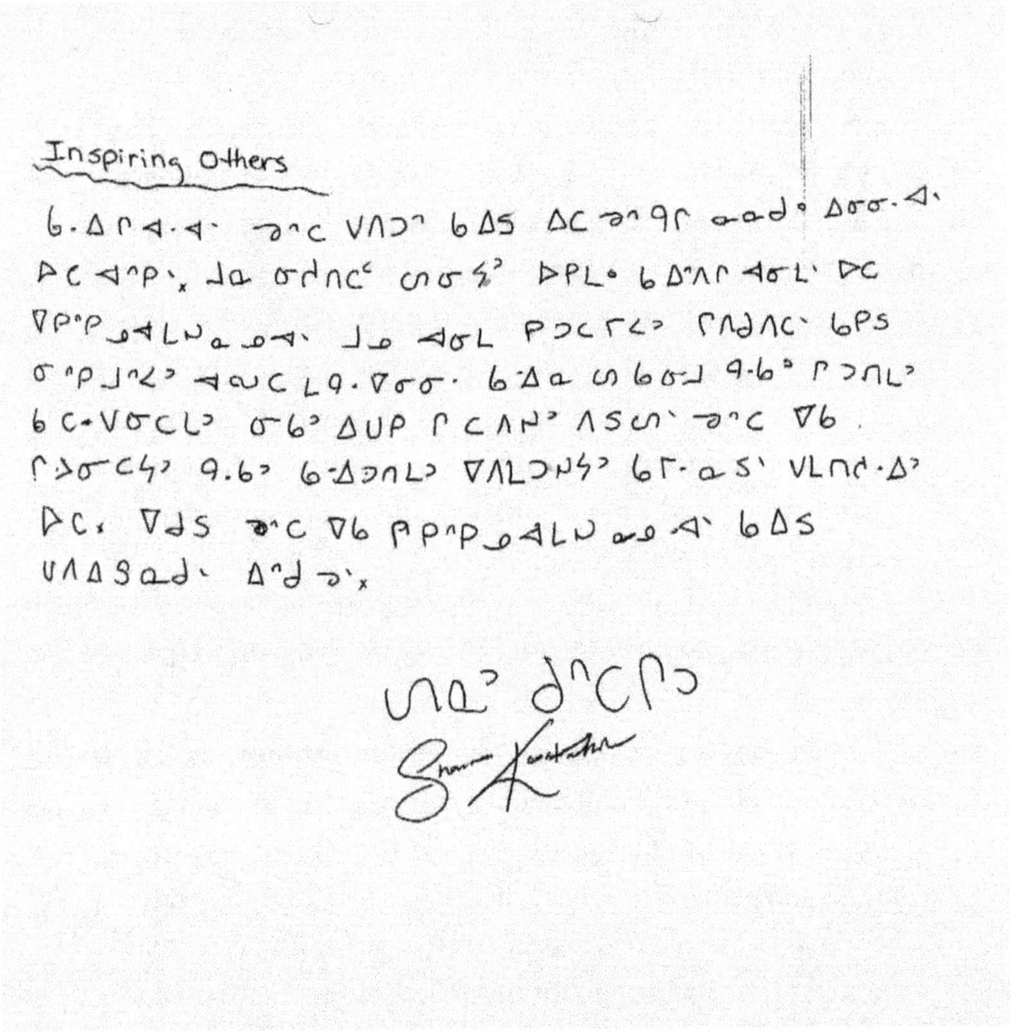

Inspiring Others

�6·ᐃ ᕐᐄ ᐊ·ᐊᐧ ᐧᔐ ᐧᐸᐧ ᔅᐃᔥ ᐊᐟᐦᕁ ᖄᐠ ᐄᐧᐧᐊ·

ᐱᓯ ᔭᐹ ᓇ ᐅᕁᓇᔅ ᐧᐅᓱᔓ ᐅᐱᒪᐧ ᖄᔭᐃᕁ ᐊᔅᐧ ᐱᓯ

(ᑌᐧᔅᔭᐧᐧᑭ ᐧᒣᐊ) ᔭ ᐊᔅᐧ ᕁᕐᔓᔭᐧ ᕐᔓᐧᔭᐧ ᖄᐸᔅ

A page from Shannen's letter for the International Peace Prize nomination, written in Cree syllabics

132

Shannen breathed a sigh of relief that Cindy mentioned the other kids. Then it hit her—the largest child rights movement in Canada—ever! Shannen's eyes opened as wide as her mouth. She saw the joy and pride on the faces of everyone in the room and threw her head back. "Holay cow!" she squealed.

The entire town was excited and proud about the accomplishments of its young people. Messages appeared on Facebook from other Aboriginal kids who were astonished that one of their own was honored.

In the last weeks of the summer, Shannen was discovering that being fourteen was different than being a happy-almost-all-the-time child. One moment she was at the top of the roller coaster and the next she was barreling down. Her family was discovering that they had to tiptoe around Shannen if she was in one of her sensitive moods. Quarrels could break out suddenly like summer storms—especially with her mother.

"You're driving me crazy, Shannen," her mother yelled in exasperation on one of those late summer days. "You never listen!" Her second teenage daughter was not nearly as quiet and obedient as her first.

"And you don't understand," Shannen yelled even louder, and burst into tears.

"Hey, hey, danis," said her mother, gathering Shannen into her arms. "What's the matter?"

Shannen cried for a long time before she could find an answer for her mother. "I'm scared, Mama. How am I going to have enough time for the school campaign, plus my schoolwork? High school will be much harder." Shannen reminded her mother about the Attawapiskat Human Rights Forum coming up in November in Toronto. "Hundreds of students will be coming from all over the province to learn about standing up for their rights. I don't want to let people down if I don't have time to help."

You're right, Shannen, high school will be more difficult," her mother said. "But you could think about asking a grade eight student to take over your role in Attawapiskat and help speak for the campaign."

Shannen's eyes lit up. "That's a great idea." Shannen knew the perfect person. "What about Chelsea?"

Her mother agreed that Chelsea would be a great help. Chelsea was very interested in the campaign. Shannen couldn't wait to ask her.

"I'm not sure," Chelsea said. She was thrilled to be asked, but she didn't know if she could handle that kind of responsibility.

Shannen knew that her friend lacked confidence. "Of course you can do it, Chels. You're a great speaker and one of the strongest people I know," she said. Then, looking straight into Chelsea's eyes, she said, "I want you to make a promise with me. We're both going to live our lives to the fullest."

Chelsea knew that Shannen was serious. "Okay, I promise, Shann."

Shannen opened her eyes wide and stared at her friend. "And you know that a promise is a promise!"

Chelsea had to laugh. "I know better than to break a promise to you!"

Shannen spent a lot of time in those last weeks with Katrina and Ocean, taking long walks and reminiscing about growing up together and imagining their futures. They sometimes ended up climbing up the church roof to sit and gaze out over the flat muskeg, to the far edges of their world.

"Remember when you brats tied me to a telephone pole and ran away and left me?" Shannen said on one of their walks, giving Katrina and Ocean her headlight glare. She imitated the police officer phoning her mother. 'Do you know your daughter is tied to a pole calling for help?'" The girls fell back laughing.

The next moment, Shannen's mood darkened. "I can't believe I'm leaving my family to live with strangers," she said, peering into the clouds.

"But Charlie isn't a stranger, and you won't be alone," Ocean said. "Serena will be with you."

Shannen also could not imagine living so far away from her friends. She would miss their sleepovers, horror movie nights, dancing, and most of all, laughing. Whenever she had problems at home, it was her friends she would run to.

"Who will I share my troubles with?" asked Shannen, glumly.

Shannen, Ocean Nakogee, and Ashley Sutherland

Shannen and Chelsea Edwards

"But ShanShann, you are the one who listens to all my problems. You are the one who encourages me to go to school when I just want to stay in bed," Katrina said.

"Katrina's right, Shann," Ocean said. "We all turn to you to whenever we need help. You are the strong one who picks us up and puts us back together. That's why you're called Dear Diary."

"You know that this is the best decision for you, Shann," said Katrina. "The high school in New Liskeard is five times bigger. You'll have so many more opportunities."

Shannen knew it was true and in her happy moments, she looked forward to the opportunities that awaited her. But the good feelings were always tempered by sadness for all the things she would have to give up. There was no turning back, though. She knew this was one of those opportunities she couldn't pass up. And she would need the best education now that she had decided on a new career—she was going to be a lawyer, like Cindy.

If only she could get the best education closer to home.

CHAPTER 18
Spreading Her Wings

"I want to tell the children to pray and be strong. To stand up for their rights because the New School Campaign is growing. There are a lot of supporters around the world."

Shannen Koostachin, 13, 2008

"The bus will be here in five minutes," urged Serena, dragging Shannen out of bed. "Get up or I'll get a bucket of cold water!"

"Okay, okay," Shannen said drowsily, as she staggered out of bed and into the bathroom.

Brit shook her head as she watched Hurricane Shannen sweep through the house, throwing on clothes, brushing her teeth while grabbing food for lunch, filling her purple travel mug with tea, and stuffing homework into her backpack. Hair and make-up were done on the bus ride to school. "It's a miracle that Shannen has never missed the bus," she marveled.

The first time she stepped through the front doors of her new school, Shannen actually broke down in tears. "I was happy and sad at the same time," she said on the phone to her mother that evening. "I felt so lucky. Everyone I passed in the halls was friendly and I felt so comfy and warm. Then I thought of the kids back home and my tears were for them—for what they were missing."

At first, Shannen and Serena found the high school work very difficult. Shannen remembered her grandfather's warnings that their elementary education would not prepare them for high school off the reserve. As Shannen told Katrina in an e-mail, "I feel like a grade four kid in a grade nine class." Shannen worried that she might never catch up, so the sisters spent most of their free time in the bedroom they shared or at the library, studying and working on homework assignments. Before long, Shannen began to feel more confident.

Homesickness was a more difficult problem to overcome. Shannen missed her family desperately and many times she phoned her mother in tears. She began to depend on Serena more than ever before. They were lucky to have each other, especially in the early days when they didn't have much time to make new friends. But spending so much time together sometimes got on their nerves and they could be very crabby with each other. They needed to make their own friends, but it wasn't easy.

Shannen felt particularly awkward and lonely during lunch period, especially if Serena had a class. When she first entered the cafeteria, hundreds of kids sat in groups at tables, laughing and talking. Everyone here was a stranger to her. Although Shannen recognized a few faces from her classes, she hadn't made any friends. She doubted that she would ever make close friends like she had back home.

Shannen missed Julius's jokes. Sometimes she'd call him just so he would make her laugh. When Shannen talked with Raven and Mickiso, she had them in stitches describing life at Charlie's house. "I can't hear myself think with all the quiet!" Shannen told them. "There's nobody around to bug me. I miss you so much, you little brats! And it's so neat and tidy here. Charlie gets upset because our clothes are piled on the floor." Compared to other rooms in the Angus home, their bedroom looked as if a bomb had exploded in it.

It wasn't too long before Shannen made friends. Another grade nine girl noticed Shannen sitting by herself at a coffee shop. Melany said, "Wacheyeh!" in East James Bay Cree. Shannen recognized her from their bus. Then Melany's friend Mallory said, "Hey! Can we sit with you?" Shannen folded easily into their group and they became true friends.

Every day, school became a little easier. Every new experience was like turning the pages of a book. Attawapiskat had been so

familiar, small, and safe. Life off the reserve was the opposite—
but exhilarating. Shannen was interested in all the new things
she was learning, and all the new opportunities that were opening up before her. She had been so frightened to take the first
steps on her journey into this larger world. Now she realized that
the path was rising to meet her. It wasn't so difficult after all.

"Hey, Kookum, guess what? I'm taking a cooking class,"
said Shannen during one of their weekly phone calls to their
grandparents. "I'm the only one who can make bannock." It
felt good to speak their language. "Serena and I have joined the
Powwow planning committee. Every member is a First Nations
student. We've lots to do to organize the Powwow in June. We're
already practicing Fancy Shawl dancing so we can perform."
Shannen knew her grandmother would be delighted. "Hundreds
of people attend the Powwows in this area."

"Powwow circles bring great tribal nations together as one.
It teaches our young about their culture," her grandmother said.

"Serena will wear the red satin regalia that Rosie's sister
sewed. It's so beautiful!" Shannen longed for regalia of her own.
She had worn shawls that Rosie had sewn for all her dancers
for the Powwows in Attawapiskat, but materials were expensive
and they had to share.

"Do you know what the Fancy Shawl dance represents,
nisom?" Shannen knew that it was a butterfly dance but she

wanted to hear Kookum explain it. "The caterpillar lives a quiet life before it encloses itself in a cocoon. Then it breaks free and blooms into a beautiful, delicate creature, gracefully floating through the sky, expressing the joy of new life. It is a dance about you, my granddaughter. It's about a young teenager growing into a woman."

Shannen felt warm all over. Living away from home had made her feel more grown up, but no one had ever called her a "woman" before. Even though Serena did her best to mother her, Shannen was spreading her wings and learning to live more independently, away from the protected shelter of her family and community. Of course it was frightening and she missed home, but Shannen was beginning to feel more comfortable and secure in her new life. She was seizing opportunities and creating a future for herself.

At the back of Shannen's mind, there was the Peace Prize. Cindy had told her it could take a few months to be decided, so she tried to chase her thoughts away, but it was difficult. She fantasized about going to the award ceremony in Europe, flying over the ocean on a jumbo jet—not the small cargo planes that flew into Attawapiskat. She would take her mother with her. Seven kids really kept her mother busy and she deserved a vacation to someplace wonderful. And Shannen fantasized about the prize money, too. She tried to calculate how many computers and books could be bought for the new school, and all the latest software games and apps. Her imaginary shopping list grew and grew until it included high-heeled shoes and aviator glasses from Europe. And shouldn't every school have a karaoke machine?

In November, Shannen and Serena were hanging out in their bedroom, totally bored, and making goofy videos with their cell-phone when they received a call from Cindy Blackstock. Serena held out the phone to her sister, but Shannen mouthed the words, "You ask her!"

Shannen jiggled and bit her fingernails. Serena asked, "Have you heard about the Peace Prize?"

Shannen read Serena's expression in an instant—disappoint-ment. She fought back tears and took the phone.

"I'm afraid that your name wasn't on the list of finalists," Cindy said. Serena sat beside her. "I know how disappointed you must feel, but you should be very proud. Think about what an inspiring role model you are, not just to Aboriginal children, but to children across the country."

"Have you heard anything about the letter to the UN yet?" asked Shannen, eager to switch subjects.

Cindy replied, "These things take a very long time, I'm afraid.

It takes even longer to get answers from the UN than from the government." Then she mentioned the Attawapiskat Human Rights Forum that was fast approaching. She and Serena had been asked to speak at the event being held in Toronto. They couldn't wait to see their friends and relatives who were also attending. "We asked Chelsea to be the emcee."

Shannen called her friend right away. "I'm so proud of you, Chels. You'll be awesome!"

"Cindy told me about the Prize," Chelsea said. "That sucks. You totally deserved it."

Shannen tried to stay lighthearted. "Hey, man, it's no big deal."

Chelsea read from the Attawapiskat Human Rights Forum program. "You, Jonah, Chris, and Solomon are the 'special guests.' I'll be speaking along with Marvin and Sky about what education is like in Attawapiskat. Your grandfather and other elders are giving speeches and prayers. Indian and Northern Affairs is supposed to send a representative too." Shannen cringed at the thought.

Later, Shannen broke the news about the prize to her dad. "That's too bad, my daughter, but we are so proud of you." He reminded her of all the notices of support on Facebook. Before bed that night, she read them again.

"This is incredible, what an inspiration."

"Hola smacks! Can you believe it? A young Native girl in Canada has been nominated for the international children's peace prize award!"

"omg!...no I can't believe it. that's amazing. I think thats the first ever young NATIVE, and GIRL ever, ever..."

That did the trick. Shannen was crying again, but this time the happy kind of tears. She had so many reasons to be proud. When I'm Prime Minister, I'll take my whole family to Europe! she joked to herself.

Aboriginal Day in Attawapiskat

CHAPTER 19
The Back of the Bus

"I would tell the children . . . to ignore people who are putting
you down. Get up and tell them what you want . . . what
you need! NEVER give up hope. Get up; pick up your books,
and GO TO SCHOOL (just not in portables)."

Shannen Koostachin, 13, 2008

When the sisters arrived in Toronto for the Human Rights
Forum, they met Cindy Blackstock. They greeted each
other like old friends, even though they had never met in person. "See all the people who care about Attawapiskat," Cindy
exclaimed as they scanned the auditorium, which was filling
with students from grade six and up from all over the province,
including reserves.

"See who doesn't care," said Shannen, scrunching her lips
in the direction of the empty chair reserved for the Indian and
Northern Affairs representative.

When it was her time to speak, Shannen described what it

was like to be schooled in portables. "You know that kids in other communities have proper schools, so you begin to feel as if you are a child who doesn't count for anything. That's why some of our students begin to give up in grade four and five. Imagine a child who feels she has no future, even at that young age."

Shannen spoke about the fearless determination in her community. "We are not going to give up. We want our younger brothers and sisters to go to school thinking that school is a time for hopes and dreams of the future. Every kid deserves this."

The high point of the day for Shannen was Serena's speech that began, "Wacheyeh Misahweh, (Hello everyone). Do you know the story of Rosa Parks in Alabama?" Serena explained that African Americans once had to sit at the back of the bus. "And then, one day, Rosa Parks sat at the front of the bus and said she wasn't going to sit at the back any longer. One person stood up for her rights and she helped change America."

Serena spoke for all First Nations children who were in portables or condemned buildings, for children being denied their most basic education rights, not just in Attawapiskat, but all across Canada. "This is the way things have been done for years in Canada—ever since the days of residential schools. It's time we stood up and fought for our rights, just like Rosa Parks. If one person can change everything, then I'm pretty sure that all the students here in this room can change the world, too." The room exploded with applause and cheers. "We need you to go out and build this campaign so that the children will finally get a better future! Meegwetch."

A woman took the microphone and addressed the Attawapiskat group, "I want you to know that you are not alone." Shannen remembered only one year before how it felt to think that no one outside their reserve knew or cared about them. Instead of feeling alone, now they were part of a wave, a wave that had gathered drops of water in its path to create a powerful force. The support of strangers was the wind that gave the wave

Shannen spoke at the Attawapiskat Human Rights Forum in Toronto, Ontario, in November of 2008.

A20 ★ TORONTO STAR ★ THURSDAY, NOVEMBER 27, 2008

NEWS > SAFETY > NATIVE ISSUES

Reserve teens want school building

Cree students tell peers from 'big comfy schools' what it's like to study in a string of portables

LOUISE BROWN
EDUCATION REPORTER

Students from "big comfy schools" across southern Ontario listened stunned yesterday to peers from a native reserve talk about what it's like to go to a school with no building — just a string of portables where mice run across the snacks, the James Bay wind blows through windows that don't close and a staggering 15 per cent of children never finish Grade 8.

"When you know other children have big comfy schools with hallways that are warm, you feel like you don't count for anything," said Shannen Koostachin of Attawapiskat, a reserve that has been waiting eight years for federal funding for a new school to replace one closed after diesel oil contaminated soil.

"That's why some of our children stop going to school in Grade 4 and 5," said the 14 year old, one of 30 students from the fly-in community who came to Toronto to share their story at a youth forum on the Attawapiskat students' plight.

More than 250 students from across southern Ontario came to the forum, co-sponsored by the Toronto Catholic District School

VINCE TALOTTA/TORONTO STAR
Serena Koostachin,16, of Attawapiskat, a northern reserve, talks to city Catholic school students yesterday.

Board and aboriginal groups, public school boards and teachers' federations. The forum host was the Ontario Institute for Studies in Education at the University of Toronto.

Not having a proper school feeds into the early dropout rate, said Attawapiskat education director John Nakogee.

"Only about 85 per cent of our children graduate from Grade 8, and I'm sure it would help to have a school building that would create a sense of family," he said.

Ottawa had long suggested it would replace the school, but last year Indian Affairs Minister Chuck Strahl said there was no money for the $30 million project. In a statement provided yesterday to the *Star*, Strahl said his department has set up a working group with the community "to develop funding options. We remain committed to working with the community to find long-term solutions to secure a permanent elementary school."

But GTA students expressed their

outrage yesterday that Attawapiskat has gone eight years without an elementary school building.

"It's unfair that they don't have a school or a playground — just a bunch of portables," said Derek Li, a Grade 9 student at Toronto's Mary Ward Catholic School, who listened to the Cree students talk about having to put their coats on to go to the gym or the library.

Serena Koostachin, 16, Shannen's older sister, said yesterday she will continue to fight for a new school.

its power. On the day of the Attawapiskat Human Rights Forum, Shannen knew in her heart that the Government of Canada could ignore them no longer.

When the sisters went home for the Christmas holidays, their suitcases crammed with Christmas presents, they felt lighter, happier. Shannen was confident that her community would soon get the school they deserved and she finally felt caught up with the other kids in her class. Shannen slid comfortably into the chaos, noise, and clutter of Christmas at the Koostachin home. Their mother had decorated the house inside, their father the outside—more lavishly than ever before. Shannen helped decorate their snowmobile for the parade. Her wrist ached at the end of the parade from waving so enthusiastically!

Shannen was eager to hear everyone's news at the Christmas Feast.

"School's not as much fun without you, sister," Ashley complained. "Remember when we photocopied our heads in grade seven?"

"I remember you were so shy when you first came to J.R.," said Shannen.

"You kept looking at me and waving," said Ashley. "You

were the first person to talk to me." Shannen felt a rush of empathy, remembering how daunting it had been last fall to face so many strangers in Timiskaming Secondary School.

Katrina told the story of the time Shannen sneaked green and purple paint from the school and the girls covered a wall with handprints. Shannen hadn't laughed so hard since the summer. It felt good to remember these times with her old friends. She had made great friends

Shannen and Ashley had been friends since they were little.

at her new school, but nothing compared to this.

When it was time to go back for school, Shannen felt pulled in two directions. How could she be looking forward to going back when she would miss these people and this place so much? Even though she knew her Atta friends were happy for her, she felt guilty about wanting to get back and hang out with her new friends. There were also the Powwows coming up and Shannen was craving dancing again. But it was bittersweet. It just did not seem fair that she was getting so much better an education at Timiskaming than her dear friends were getting at home.

CHAPTER 20
The Old Gray Ghost

"Such a situation here would be dealt with immediately and no child would ever be put in such a dangerous position as to sit in a classroom or play in a schoolyard steps away from a toxic-waste site."

Brenda Stewart, Toronto teacher, 2009

Hi danis, The principal sent us home early today because of the cold—minus 50 according to the wind chill. The students couldn't concentrate and the pipes froze. Hi-ho mistahey, Mama Bear.

Shannen read out the message to Serena. When the sisters felt homesick, they went to the computer to catch up on news of family and friends. If they got the timing just right, they could sometimes do a live chat.

"That's one thing I don't miss about being away from Atta in January," said Serena. "The cold!"

Her mother continued, "We received boxes of books from a boy named Andrew who asked for books for First Nation communities instead of money or presents. He saw your video and decided to send them to J.R. Nakogee this year."

"Does he know that the school doesn't have a library? ☹"

"We sent them home with the kids instead."

Shannen typed, "Is there any news about the campaign?"

"Nothing new, but the old school is being demolished in March," her mother replied.

"Finally!" said Shannen, angrily, thinking how wrong it was that there still wasn't anything to replace it.

"Health Canada checked the health and safety of the portables and found carbon-dioxide levels three times the acceptable limit. The teacher asked if that was why her class was drowsy and complained of headaches. The inspector told her to turn on the bathroom fan and open a window. Imagine that! In minus 30 temperatures!!"

"Just what the kids need—more cold air!" Shannen wrote back.

In March, Shannen received a parcel. "My regalia!" she cried to Serena, tearing off the wrapping. She lifted the soft blue satin

Serena and Shannen in their Fancy Shawl regalia

shawl to her cheek. "It's beautiful! It's forget-me-not blue." Shannen ran her finger along the black embroidered eagles and stars and let the silky ribbons slip through her fingers like water.

Serena read the note, "Dear Shannen, Your mother asked me to make this for your birthday. She wanted you to have it early to wear at the Powwow. I hope you like it." Shannen was thrilled but not entirely surprised by the gift. Ever since Serena had received her Fancy Shawl regalia from Katrina's aunt last year, Shannen had dropped hints at every opportunity.

"Stop bouncing around the room and try it on," Serena cried.

Shannen gazed at her reflection in the mirror. She stood taller, prouder—as if the regalia had somehow made her a better person. She pulled her thick black hair off her forehead, imagining a braid falling down her back. Serena said, "You have time to grow your bangs by June, Shann."

"I can't wait to show everyone in Atta."

"But you're already packed and ready to go, and there's no room in your bag," Serena said, laughing. They weren't leaving for almost a week. but Serena loved to tease her sister for being an over-eager beaver to get home for March Break.

The following Saturday, the sisters took a train to Moosonee where they met their father and Raven for the four-hour drive on the ice road up the coast. While her sisters slept in the back seat, Shannen chattered away like a chipmunk. Her father laughed. "I brought Raven to keep me company on the drive and I almost forgot that she was there! And you, my daughter, have not stopped talking."

"Okay, Pops. What's new?"

"Well, Chelsea's left for Toronto where she's giving a speech at a conference," her father answered. "More and more schools and universities are pledging support and students keep writing letters. School boards, teachers' federations, churches, and union workers are helping, too. Everything is real good, danis, so you don't need to worry."

Shannen scowled. "Real good would be a real school. So, how's the demolition going? Did the ghosts get angry for disturbing their old place?"

"You know, Shannen, the school isn't all that old to us. Your mother remembers when it was brand new. She says kids used to run and slide down the halls. The poor teachers had a tough time training them to walk in the halls and sit quietly at their desks." Her father smiled. "I didn't come to J.R. until grade eight, but I thought it was a great school. The whole community was proud of J.R. Nakogee."

Shannen had blurry memories of her days in kindergarten—the halls decorated with Valentine hearts, visiting other classrooms dressed in Halloween costumes, singing "Jingle Bells" in front of a packed gym.

"We have so many wonderful memories of that school. When Julius and Serena went to school on their first day, they cried and we cried. Then when it was your turn, danis, you ran off happily and didn't look back!" A cloud passed over his eyes. "When the walls came down, it was heartbreaking, especially for your mother."

Shannen was so used to hearing—and talking—about the bad things about the old school. People hardly ever talked about all the good things it stood for. She had almost forgotten that there were happy memories, too.

The demolition of J.R. Nakogee School made the older residents sad.

"So, is the school completely gone?" Shannen asked.

Her father squinted his eyes against the blinding glare of the ice. "The building is gone, but there's still a big hole. When they uncovered the basement, we started smelling diesel fuel. Parents and teachers were really worried." He sounded worried, too. "People complained of headaches. Some kids fell asleep at their desks."

"That sounds dangerous," Shannen shrieked, startling her sisters awake.

Raven knew right away that they were talking about the smell. "Oh, Shannen, it's disgusting. Some kids barfed!"

"We kept the students inside for recess," their father said. "The workers wore masks and coveralls but the kids weren't protected. The government is testing the site but the reports say that there is nothing to worry about."

"Then why are the workers wearing coveralls and face masks?" asked Serena.

"I'm only a kid, but something that smells that bad can't be good," Shannen said, angrily.

As soon as they arrived home, Shannen phoned Katrina. "Oh, Shann, it's awful. The wind has blown the red dust from the site into our yard. It's making me dizzy and sick to my stomach. We were getting diarrhea, even the baby. My brother has a gross rash under his arms—it smells like rotten meat!"

Shannen couldn't believe what she was hearing. Her cousin was in such a state. She tried to sound positive. "Dad's going to a community meeting to talk about closing the schools."

Her father looked worn out after he came home from the six-hour meeting. "The community doesn't believe the air quality tests. They're worried about the toxic debris being dumped right near our water. They want to close the schools and evacuate seven hundred residents."

"How will I graduate from high school?" Julius asked. His question made Shannen wonder about Chelsea graduating from grade eight.

"That has not been decided yet, but don't worry, nobody's forgetting you guys."

Her father tried to reassure his family that everything would work out.

Shannen pretended to believe her father, but inside she doubted that things would work out. Only days before, she was so happy to be coming home. Now she was angry and frustrated and couldn't wait to get away from the foul odour to go back to their clean and safe school. This made her feel selfish and disloyal. She thought about the number of times she encouraged her friends to never give up hope. Now hope was slipping away and she didn't know how to get it back.

After March Break, the sisters tried to keep up with news from home. When the girls read the newspaper headline, "Attawapiskat declares state of emergency," they stared at each other, feeling helpless. They knew an evacuation would cost millions of dollars. "It says here that INAC won't agree to an evacuation because according to their tests, nothing is wrong. I just don't understand," said Shannen. "If the government says there is no danger, why are people getting sick?"

"This is a very, very dangerous situation," Charlie Angus said after he returned from a visit to Attawapiskat. He told them about an independent report that identified chemicals known to cause leukemia, bone marrow damage, and kidney failure.

Suddenly, Shannen was seized with fear. One young student at J.R. had leukemia already. She remembered when Dallas had a life-threatening illness as a baby. That was the most scared Shannen had ever been. She couldn't bear her family facing another nightmare like that. She began to wonder why there seemed to be so much less sickness here in New Liskeard. Before moving here, she thought all the illnesses back home were just a normal part of life and she felt lucky to be one of the healthy ones. But why did so many people in Attawapiskat have asthma and cancer and other health problems? Could poisoned air and water be the reason?

She wanted to jump on a plane to get back home. But how?

A flight cost over a thousand dollars. She looked at her bulging backpack—a reminder of all the homework she had to do. But how could she concentrate with so much on her mind?

Shannen tried to hide her worries from friends at school, but Melany and Mallory noticed a change. They had grown to love Shannen's bubbly and cheerful nature, her crazy sense of humor, her zest for life and all its gifts and opportunities. Now they could see that Shannen was walking in dark shadows cast from problems at home. She was touchy, especially if her friends complained about their parents or their school. She'd pounce like a cat. "Do you have any idea how lucky you are?"

Chelsea kept her up to date with campaign news but Shannen could sense that she was getting discouraged at the government's lack of action, as well. "The Students-Helping-Students campaign is really growing off the reserve, but our leaders have more important problems to cope with right now," Chelsea said. Shannen tried to hide her doubts from her friend. "I can't wait to get out of Attawapiskat and into the fresh air at our camp. I missed our holiday in March because of the conference, so I'm really looking forward to a break," said Chelsea. Shannen was silent. And then Chelsea felt badly. "Sorry, Shann, I forgot that your school doesn't have the Goose Break."

"I wish I could go on the hunt," Shannen said, miserably. April was so dull and boring and ugly in New Liskeard. She missed the fresh spring breeze blowing through the grasses in Akimiski and the unbroken expanse of muskeg and sky that seemed to reach forever. She yearned for the taste of fresh fish caught through a hole in the ice and goose roasted over an open fire. Although when she first moved here, she couldn't get enough coffee and doughnuts, now she'd much rather have tea bloss and bannock. Shannen couldn't wait to speak with her family and hear all about the hunt.

Her father called as soon as they arrived home. "Danis, there has been a terrible hunting accident," her father said. "It's Brendon. Shannen, he's home with the Creator now."

Brendon Kioke loved canoeing at Camp Wenonah.

CHAPTER 21
Forget Me Not

Realize that we as human beings have been put on this Earth for only a short time and that we must use this time to gain wisdom, knowledge, respect, and the understanding for all human beings, since we are all relatives.

Cree Proverb

When Shannen came back to school from the reserve for the second time that spring, she needed solace from her grief. She found it in dancing. When she practiced her Fancy Shawl dance for the upcoming Powwows, Shannen felt as though she were in a trance. She was a butterfly fluttering around the forget-me-nots in a field, hovering above sadness, anger, and disappointment. There was no accident, no government official breaking promises, no contamination, no worry. Her heart healed.

Shannen and Serena were invited to dance in a Powwow in nearby Quebec. When they finished performing, they were surprised to see Melany. "You danced so beautifully—so wild and free!" Melany was from the Matachewan Band but she had never had an interest in learning this part of her culture until she saw Shannen dance. "Can you teach me?"

Shannen felt honored and excited to be able to share this part of herself with her friend. At Timiskaming Secondary School's annual Powwow, Shannen looked directly into Melany's eyes. "You must promise me that next year you will dance with me." Melany promised, and Shannen had a feeling Melany wasn't the type to break a promise.

Not long after, just before the sisters left New Liskeard for the summer break, they were asked to speak at a labor rally in support of their campaign. Serena spoke first about their sadness of leaving their home to get a better education. "Shannen and I sometimes get this insecure feeling because our parents aren't there."

Then Shannen gripped the microphone. "I want to tell you what it is like to never have the chance to feel educated." Tears welled up unexpectedly, and she was unable to continue.

Serena finished the speech. "We've been fighting for thirty years, now, and nothing has ever happened."

Afterwards, Serena hugged her sister. "I couldn't help thinking about last year," Shannen told her. "I really thought that something would happen. I was just a naïve kid." Shannen no longer felt like that elementary school child. A year had made a big difference. She felt like she had lost some of her innocence. Shannen was not ready to give up, but she was ready to go home. Spending time with her friends and family would renew her spirit.

Shannen tried to enjoy a carefree summer, but soon after she arrived in Attawapiskat, the sewage system failed and flooded eight homes. The Koostachins were spared, but in this close community, everyone was connected in some way to the ninety people affected. Other homes were already overcrowded and there was no place for them to go. Many had to be evacuated. People worried about what would happen to the evacuees when the band's money ran out and they had to return home.

Katrina's mother, Rosie, started a Facebook page to try to encourage people from outside to donate to the homeless. "We're receiving food, blankets, and other household necessities," Katrina told Shannen. "Some people have offered to fly in the aid for the community."

Ocean Nakogee and
Katrina Koostachin

Even though people were pulling together to help, anger and frustration swirled like funnel clouds throughout the reserve. This seemed like one crisis too many for the residents of Attawapiskat to handle.

Shannen said to Katrina, "The government provides aid to people in other countries who are facing hardships like this. Why won't they help their own people?"

The news from Attawapiskat just seemed to go from bad to worse. During the Human Rights conference only one year before, Shannen had felt that she was riding the crest of a wave. Now, she felt as if the wave had crashed to the shore and lost all of its power. Since then her community had suffered through the disastrous demolition, the loss of a beloved child, and the sewage failure. Now winter had arrived, and people were still homeless.

Shannen had agreed to be the guest speaker at the Ontario Federation of Labor conference in November, but she was in no mood to deliver the same message she had given so many times before. Shannen remembered what the National Chief had said, "Canadians don't know what is happening here. They don't know that kids are being mistreated."

When Shannen took the microphone in front of the auditorium of full of labor leaders, more than ever, she wanted Canadians to be aware of what was happening out of their sight. Shannen ended her speech with an emotional plea. "Children shouldn't have to fight for their rights. We have to fix this. It's not right."

The audience came to their feet and applauded wildly. One delegate stepped up to the microphone and said, "If we can help New Orleans rebuild after Hurricane Katrina, we should be able to head up north and build a school in Attawapiskat."

Another said, "Canadians must replace passivity with action. Our citizens can't be indifferent to injustice."

Shannen noticed that this time, it was the members of the audience who were in tears.

Jerrod Kolenski, a student at Clarke Rd. Secondary School, won first prize in the Ontario Secondary School Teachers' Federation poster contest.

CHAPTER 22
The Journey of Hope

"I have no place where I can stay on my own. I miss my home. Since I have been in Cochrane, all I do is sit inside, not like before where I used to do things inside the house as soon as morning would break. I feel like a prisoner."

Sophie Spence, 68, 2009

"You're not going to believe this," Shannen said to Serena, as she read her mother's e-mail message. "Sophie Spence is walking to Timmins!" Shannen felt her heart tug. Sophie had sung at Brendon's memorial. "She's been walking for over a week."

"What?" screeched Serena. "Sophie? Why on earth..."

"She's protesting. She's calling it her 'Journey of Hope.'"

And just like that, Shannen began to laugh. It all just seemed so comical all of a sudden. Sophie had two artificial knees. Timmins was 100 miles (160 km) away from Cochrane, where she had been staying since the evacuation. Serena caught

Shannen's contagious laughter and soon the girls were out of control, tears streaming down their faces.

"Why are we laughing?" gasped Serena, trying to catch her breath. "An elder walking in the dead of winter isn't funny, Shann."

"I know it's not funny," cried Shannen, gulping deep breaths. "It's not funny at all!" Sophie had lived in a motel after her home was flooded. "I don't think there's much hope for her Journey of Hope," Shannen's voice grew louder. "She should call it her Journey of Hopeless!"

Serena looked at her sister strangely. Shannen's hands covered her face and her shoulders heaved up and down. Serena could not tell if she was laughing or crying. Then Shannen threw herself on the bed and buried her head in the pillow.

"Hey, hey, nimeem," Serena whispered, slipping beside her

"I ask you to stand up for what is right, what is fair, and what Canada has always stood for. As a country, we are known internationally for our altruism and hospitality. What does it say to the rest of the world if we cannot provide for those within our own borders? The current situation in Attawapiskat taints Canada's upstanding reputation and I am losing faith in our government."

OSSTF first prize letter winner Tom Grainger

and drawing Shannen near. "It's okay."

"It's not okay!" Shannen said between sobs. "It's not okay! Why should an elder have to walk for two weeks in the freezing cold winter so people will pay attention to our problems? Why? She'll just get ignored the same way we have been ignored. Why should children give up their grad trip and make speeches and more speeches. Nothing ever changes. Nothing ever makes a difference." Shannen drew her knees to her chest. "I give up, Serena. Winning this fight is impossible."

"Nothing's impossible, ShanShann. You said it yourself," Serena said, through her own tears. "Remember last week you spoke at that labor conference? Charlie said you blew the crowd away. You convinced everyone there to help us. You can't give up now."

"But we said exactly the same thing a whole year ago. We

> "These are children of our beautiful land, and they are as much deserving of an education as anyone else. I believe our education in Canada is what makes us such a wonderful and strong country, and without it these students will never get to experience the power and freedom that comes with knowledge and education."
> Third place prize winner
> Samantha Skinner

were sure that the government would promise a new school. It was just a matter of time." Shannen's despair turned to anger. "And look what happened—nothing. In fact, the situation in Attawapiskat is worse. Much worse!"

Serena held Shannen tighter, just like her mother used to do when she was younger. "Do you remember when I felt like giving up?" Serena repeated her father's words, "You get up, pick up your books, and keep walking in your moccasins."

"I'm tired of walking, nimis." Shannen shuddered. Serena pulled a blanket over her.

"I know, ShanShann. Moonaneh, gawenah mateh," don't worry, don't cry. "Papa also told us that we should pray." For a long time the sisters remained silent.

"What you need is a bedtime story, Shann." Serena leaned over to reach a large envelope next to the bed. It contained the winning entries from the Voices of Attawapiskat Campaign,

"The children are the future of Canada, we are all special. One of us might cure cancer or be the next Prime Minister. . . . You wouldn't be in your position today if you hadn't gone to school and worked hard. I am asking that you give the children of Attawapiskat a chance at education too."

Third place prize winner Grace Tang

a letter and poster contest for Thames Valley School Board students. "Listen to this one. 'I would just like to thank you for taking the time to read all of our letters...' I wonder how many letters the government has had to read by now."

Shannen managed a weak smile. "I hope they have to build a portable to store them."

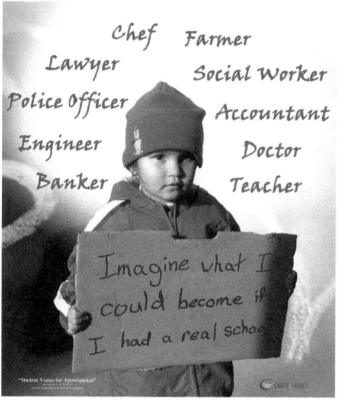

Kayla Stewart from Laurier Secondary School won the poster contest's second place prize.

Fight for a school for the children of Attawapiskat

CHAPTER 23
The Butterfly Dance

"It is unacceptable in Canada that First Nations children cannot attend a safe and healthy school. Now is the time for fairness, justice, and equity. Now is the time to realize Shannen's Dream."

Shawn A-in-chut Atleo, National Chief, Assembly of First Nations, 2010

S hannen woke up the next morning, groggy and headachy, still dressed in yesterday's clothes. Her untouched home-work glared at her. Before she could announce that she was not going to school, her older sister pulled back the covers and insisted that she get up.

"Ugh!" Shannen grunted, as she looked at her puffy eyes in the mirror.

"What good will it do just to sit at home and be miserable, ShanShann?"

As soon as Shannen climbed on the bus, Melany could see that her friend was having a bad day. She had no idea what to do or say to make Shannen feel better. Later, Mallory suggested that they go Christmas shopping at the mall after school. She knew how much Shannen loved Christmas.

"Maybe tomorrow," said Shannen weakly. "I've got lots to do at home." What she really needed most of all was to hear her parents' voices.

"How far is Sophie now?" Shannen asked her dad that night.

"She's over half way. She's doing real good. We're all proud of old Sophie."

Shannen couldn't hide her tears from her father so she told him about her breakdown.

"You have accomplished so much, danis," said her father, gently. "Maybe now is the time for you to focus on other things— your schoolwork, your dancing, your friends, and all the things that give you comfort."

"But what if our dream for a school—"

Her father cut her off. "There you go worrying about 'what ifs' Shannen—remember, 'ifs' might never happen. Don't hold yourself responsible for the inaction of others."

Shannen knew that her father was right. But her heart still felt heavy.

"Remember the Seven Grandfathers are always behind you to support you, no matter how bad things seem. Just remember what's important—your family," her father said. "Your family will get you through times of trouble. They will always be there for you."

Shannen thought about her grandparents and great-grandmother and the gift of their wisdom, and especially her parents, her brothers and sisters, and all her uncles and aunts and cousins. I am lucky, she thought.

Shannen thought about her friends, too. Instead of growing apart as she had feared, living far away from home had drawn her childhood friends closer, into an unbreakable bond for life. And as she walked forward into her future, her heart was making room for new friends.

"You are the lucky one, Shannen. You have the opportunity to have a good education in a good school. You have a bright future ahead." Shannen could hear her father's loving smile through the phone. It was contagious.

"Serena and I want to dance for Kookum and Mooshoom in our regalia," she said.

"They will be very proud," her father said. "We all are."

The following day, Shannen spotted an empty seat on a bench in the center of the mall and flopped down with her dollar-store bags at her feet. Melany and Mallory said in unison, "Lucky you!" Exhausted, they joined Shannen's bags and sat on the floor.

"I'm pooped!" groaned Mallory.

"Me, too," said Shannen. Melany and Mallory enjoyed seeing their friend in such a good mood. Shannen loved everything about Christmas shopping—the lame music, the cheesy decorations, the sweltering mall, the crowds, even the meltdowns of children and their crabby parents.

The friends took a timeout to consult their lists. "Omigawd, Shannen! You have, like, a hundred presents to buy!"

Shannen grinned. "Not quite."

Beep!

Shannen fumbled in her purse for her phone. When she finally retrieved it, she stared at the screen for what seemed like several minutes. Then she lowered her head and drew her knees up to her chest, wrapping her arms around her legs tightly. Mallory and Melany exchanged concerned glances. The people who were sitting on either side of Shannen left abruptly.

Her friends slid in beside her. "What's the matter?" Melany asked, tentatively, afraid something terrible had happened.

Shannen slowly unwrapped herself, dropping her feet gently to the floor. She gracefully stretched her arms out wide and lifted her chin forward as if she were a bird about to take flight. Then she crouched slightly and began tapping one foot up and down

Shannen Koostachin loved Fancy Shawl dancing in her regalia.

as if in time to a drumbeat, and then the other, up and down, so lightly that it looked as if her feet weren't even touching the floor.

Mallory stared at her friend like she had finally snapped. A Powwow was one thing, but here they were in the middle of a crowded mall, two weeks before Christmas. She wasn't really going to dance, was she?

Melany just smiled and watched.

Shannen's arms were wings. She floated like a butterfly fluttering near the grass.

"What on Earth was in that message?" asked Mallory, shaking her head. She picked up the phone and read: "Attawapiskat wins!"

Epilogue
Shannen's Dream

"Shannen was an ordinary individual who found the strength to persevere and endure in spite of an overwhelming obstacle-taking the stand to fight for Native rights. As Shannen said, 'Thinking will not overcome fear, but action will.' She took action and shared her faith in what she had always believed was right. She became a shining light and such a big help to others in our community. And now the broken pieces to the heart of Attawapiskat have healed. Thanks to her example, we can become the solution. We can put words into action. And we can finally make dreams into reality."

Keisha Iahtail, 14, Timmins

Shannen returned to New Liskeard after the winter holiday break at home happy and proud that the government had finally agreed to build a school. She continued to practice her Fancy Shawl dancing and was thrilled to be chosen the lead dancer at her school's Powwow in early June. Shannen's grades continued to improve and her parents rewarded her for all her success with a trip to Ottawa with their good family friend, Rosa Thornton. It was a gift that her parents would always regret.

On the way home from Ottawa on May 31, 2010, the minivan Shannen was in collided with a transport truck. Shannen Noella Jane Koostachin passed away on June 1. She was fifteen years old. Rosa Thornton also died.

Katrina, and her grade eight class, had just arrived in Toronto for their much anticipated grad trip when they received news of the tragedy. They returned home immediately to share their grief with loved ones.

Shannen's closest friends met at Chris's house. His grandfather gathered them into a healing circle and offered this explanation, "Some children are sent to Earth for a special reason—to teach us. Such a child may only be with us for a brief time. When their purpose in life is fulfilled, the Creator calls them to return to the heavens. Shannen was an Okimaw. She taught many people. Her teachings will always guide us. Her spirit will always be with us."

Shannen was laid to rest in her forget-me-not blue regalia in Attawapiskat. Later, she was given her spirit name, *Wawahtay Eskwoh*, Northern Lights Woman, taken from Cree teaching, "Respect the northern lights for they are the spirits of those who have gone before, dancing."

When Shannen passed into the spirit world, her friends and family wanted to honor her memory by continuing the fight for equality for children across Canada. In October 2010, Charlie Angus introduced a motion in the House of Commons called Shannen's Dream (Motion 571) to address the underfunding of First Nations schools. "...From the ashes of her devastating loss, a renewed sense of activism is emerging among First Nations youth in the North. Shannen has inspired other youth to believe in the future and become active to make a difference in the future of their communities."

In November 2010 on Shannen's behalf, her family accepted a human rights award from the Canadian Coalition for the Rights of the Child. After the presentation, Chelsea Edwards spoke as

A roadside memorial for Shannen and Rosa Thornton

the new ambassador for the Shannen's Dream Campaign. Here is part of her speech:

"Let me tell you about my good friend Shannen Koostachin. She was inspirational to me. We both shared the same dream. We both wanted to be lawyers. For her I will fulfill that dream and Shannen's dream to get a new school.

"Shannen said that we shouldn't have to beg for equal rights. She believed that there was no reason for children to be forgotten because Canadians pride themselves on looking out for other people no matter where in the world they live. But people need

Andrew, Serena, and Jenny accepted
Shannen's Human Rights Award after her death.

to know what is happening on our reserves across Canada. It's not right. We need to change this. We need to make a difference. That is why we are here today to launch Shannen's Dream. This one's for you, girl.

"Shannen's Dream is about inspiring our Aboriginal students. One spark can light a fire inside every Aboriginal student. It's not just about the students in Attawapiskat. It's about freedom, equality, and justice for children in every reserve across Canada. Today I ask for your support. Shannen said we could change the world if we tried. We can do that hand in hand as we stand together shoulder to shoulder and say 'We can do it.'

"Let's make her dream become a reality. For those of you who want to make a difference. Join us. Stand with us. Let's make the change right now!"

Chelsea Edwards spoke to students at Elgin Street Elementary School. From left: John B. Nakogee, Pacificia Nakogee, Chelsea, Chief Theresa Spence, Terry Downey, and Summer Mudd.

Historical Note

Shannen's ancestors, the Mushkegowuk or "Swampy Cree," hunted, trapped, and fished in and around the floodplains of James Bay for so long that the water and bush were part of their spirit. In the warm weather, they set up tipis at the mouth of the Attawapiskat River and prepared fish, berries, and game for the harsh winter ahead. Some ventured west, to trade for pemmican, or south, to trade with tribes who grew corn, beans, and squash.

When the Cree encountered the British explorer Henry Hudson, it was the beginning of a trading relationship with the English and French—*Wemistukuushuu*—that lasted for three centuries. The new settlers built trading posts where Aboriginals exchanged food, pelts, and guide services for items of steel (axes, guns, traps, and pots), blankets, clothing, and flour. The Native people helped the Europeans survive the harsh winters and provided illness remedies. Tragically, European diseases would eventually wipe out most of the Aboriginal population.

Although Europeans considered them "savages," the original people were organized into confederations with their own languages and unique cultures. A Creator was central to their spirituality and they believed in protecting the sacred land for future generations. Each member of a band was valued, respected, and cared for, unlike the European class society that denied rights to women and the poor.

When Canada became a country in 1867, more immigrants arrived to build a stronger nation. The rich natural resources in the north promised jobs in mining, logging, farming, and construction. To obtain the rights to these resources, the government needed to negotiate treaties with the original settlers.

A Cree family at the turn of the 20th century

During this time, the Cree understood that their way of life was changing. Many gave up their nomadic ways to settle around the trading posts. People began to die of starvation and disease when animals in the vicinity became over-trapped. To protect their children's future, the Anishinaabe (Northern Ojibwe) and Cree bands signed the Kih-chi-itwe-win, known as The James Bay Treaty Number 9, with the Canadian government. In exchange for a vast territory of approximately half the size of the province of Alberta, the Indians were given money, medicine, schools, and relief to help them survive. The elders believed that their hunting, fishing, and trapping rights would be protected, and the land and resources shared. Since the signing, many have argued that the terms were not properly translated orally.

Canada provided education by forcing young children to attend residential schools, deliberately placed far from their families so that some could not return home for years. The staff's duty was to civilize the "savages" by prohibiting the use of their language and culture. Christianity replaced native spirituality. Many children were neglected and abused physically and emotionally. More than half died running away, or from illness and suicide. When J.R. Nakogee School opened in Attawapiskat, families were overjoyed that finally children could attend school in their community.

As trading posts closed, hunters and trappers lost their

means of making a living. More people moved into Attawapiskat. Government money was not sufficient to cover daily expenses. Unsafe water and overcrowded homes caused ill health. The psychological scars of residential school began to surface. Survivors lacked parenting skills. Loss of self-esteem, loss of culture, loss of hope for their future, led to depression, suicide, and substance abuse.

In Attawapiskat, education is seen as the way to surmount these problems. Attawapiskat First Nation wants its children to get the best education possible to succeed in the future. The seeds of hope planted by the children of this community have begun to take root. In June 2011, a report entitled Our Dreams Matter, Too was submitted to the United Nations Committee on the Rights of the Child. The new school, with a playground and athletic fields, is scheduled to open in 2013, thirty-four years after the diesel fuel contamination. Children have suggested that the school be named after Shannen Koostachin. Shannen's Dream continues to grow. For more information go to www.shannensdream.ca.

Timeline

40–70,000 BCE – People migrate to the northern hemisphere across land and sea.

13,000 BCE – Settlers live around James Bay after the glaciers recede from the last Ice Age.

1000 – Viking explorers arrive on the east coast.

1400 – European fishermen trade with Aboriginal people for furs.

1534 – Jacques Cartier, who is welcomed by Aboriginals eager to trade, claims the 'New Land' for France.

1603 – Samuel de Champlain signs treaties with tribes to settle along the St. Lawrence River in return for military assistance against the Iroquois.

1611 – Henry Hudson meets a Cree hunter who offers pelts as trade for gifts.

1670 – The Hudson's Bay Trading Company is formed.

1754 – The British promise that Iroquois lands will be protected after forming an alliance against the French.

1763 – Great Britain's Royal Proclamation recognizes First Nations' ownership of their land.

1830 – The Indian Department sets up a system of reserves in Upper Canada (Ontario).

1867 – The new Dominion of Canada claims jurisdiction over Indians and their lands without consultation.

1876 – The Indian Act of Canada, or "Acte des Sauvages," defines who has legal Indian status.

1884 – The Indian Act bans Potlatches. Later revisions ban regalia, traditional dances, and other sacred ceremonies, and prohibits the formation of political groups.

1905 – Government Treaty No. 9 is signed by the Ojibwe and Cree.

1930 – Residential school is compulsory for children between the ages of seven and 15.

1945 – Aboriginals who volunteered for World War II lose their Indian status and are not allowed housing loans given to non-Native veterans.

1947 – Parliament consults Aboriginal leaders, for the first time, for their views on Indian policies.

1951 – The ban on traditional ceremonies is removed.

1960 – Indians are given equal voting rights in federal elections.

1968 – The first Native person is elected to Parliament.

1981 – Aboriginal people protest the exclusion of their rights from the Canadian constitution. The next year The Charter of Rights and Freedoms protects existing Aboriginal and treaty rights.

1985 – The Indian Act ends discrimination against women. Previously, women lost their status if they married a non-Native.

1996 – The last residential school closes.

2007 – Canada is one of four countries to vote against the UN Declaration on the Rights of Indigenous Peoples.

2008 – The Truth and Reconciliation Commission listens to the stories of former residential school students, and on June 11, the prime minister formally apologizes for the harm done to First Nations familes.

2010 – Canada endorses the UN Declaration on the Rights of Indigenous Peoples.

Glossary

Aboriginal: Collective name for Original Peoples. The Canadian constitution recognizes three groups of Aboriginal Peoples: Indians (commonly referred to as First Nations), Métis and Inuit. These are three distinct peoples with unique histories, languages, cultural practices, and spiritual beliefs. More than one million people in Canada identify themselves as Aboriginal.

Apartheid: Deliberate discrimination based on race. It was used in South Africa to describe the legal system of denying citizens rights based on their skin color. Some claim that apartheid was influenced by the Canadian Indian Act.

Assembly of First Nations (AFN): The national voice of more than 600 First Nations communities in Canada. It negotiates with the Government of Canada on things such as the right to self-government and equitable sharing of lands and resources. www.afn.ca

Assimilation: A government policy aimed to encourage Aboriginals to leave behind their traditional cultures and become 'civilized.'

Blind: A screen made of tree boughs and grasses to hide hunters

Convention on the Rights of the Child: The United Nations, deciding that children needed special protection, declared that all children have basic

Blind

human rights regardless of race, sex, religion, culture, or any other status.

Dreamcatcher: A hanging willow hoop, on which is woven a loose web to catch bad dreams, which are then destroyed by the dawn.

Fancy Shawl Dance: Dancers wear beautiful regalia of brightly colored satin, ribbon, and organza adorned with appliqué, and a beaded cape, leggings, moccasins, hairpieces, and jewelry.

Feast: An important Cree tradition, Feasts represent the relationship between animals and humans and show the respect for animals who have given themselves for the benefit of the people. All food from the Feast is considered sacred, and must not be wasted in any way.

Grass Dance: Dancers flatten the grass with their feet where Feasts and special ceremonies are to take place. In some regions, the Grass Dance was a ceremonial healing dance intended to doctor a sick child who was too weak to move.

Indian Act: Enacted by Canada's Parliament in 1876, the act provides a legal definition of "Indian" and determines the rights of status (registered) Indians in Canada. Several revisions were made over time to increase their civil rights, but the act still restricts the right of Native communities to govern themselves.

The International Children's Peace Prize: Awarded annually to a child who has devoted a lot of his or her energy to improving the rights of children. www.kidsrights.org

INAC: Indian and Northern Affairs Canada, recently changed to Aboriginal Affairs and Northern Development Canada, is a federal ministry responsible for education, health, and safety of the First Nations. Its mandate is to protect the environment from pollution on reserve lands, and provide safe and reliable drinking water. It provides social programs, housing, help for persons with disabilities, and income assistance. www.ainc-inac.gc.ca

Kara Shisheesh Jingle dancing

Jingle Dress: Made from multi-colored fabric decorated with more than 100 tin cones, originally made from tobacco can lids, that create a jingling sound as the dancer moves.

Jingle Dance: originated with the Ojibwe and is characterized by light footwork danced close to the ground. The dancer moves in a pattern, her feet never cross, and she does not dance backward or turn a complete circle.

Medicine Wheel: Tool for teaching individuals the traditional view of what it means to be Aboriginal and their interrelatedness to all creations. The circle is divided into four parts, each representing an eternal element of life; spiritual, mental, emotional, physical; earth, wind, fire, water; north, south, east, west; winter, spring, summer, fall; childhood, adolescence, adulthood, old age, etc. All Medicine Wheels include white, yellow, and red, but Cree teachings have blue or green in place of black.

Muskeg: Bog land described as a soggy blanket of decayed peat moss and leaves that covers much of northern North America.

Pemmican: Preserved food made from mixing lean meat dried over fire and pounded together with fat.

Regalia: Traditional clothing used for ceremonial occasions.

Seven Grandfathers: Seven powerful spirits whose responsibility it is to show people how to live a life of goodness in harmony with nature.

S'mores: Toasted marshmallows, sandwiched with chocolate between Graham Wafers.

Smudge: Sweetgrass or cedar, burned to purify people or places.

Spirit Name: Every Cree is entitled to a unique name for his or her spirit. It is passed down by the person's spirit protector, often in a dream, to an elder or medicine person at the request of the parents.

Sweatlodge: A structure heated by pouring water over hot stones to purify occupants by making them sweat.

Tea Bloss: A tea made from the leaves and clusters of white flower blossoms of a plant that grows in muskeg.

United Nations: A collection of countries working together for peace. It was founded in 1945 after World War II to avoid wars between countries.

Glossary of Cree words*

* Spellings and meanings may vary from place to place

Ahtawspiskatowi ininiwak (Attawapiskat): people of the parting of the rocks

Danis: my daughter

Eh heh: yes

Jaban: great-grandmother

Kih-chi-itwe-win: The Great Declaration or Word (James Bay Treaty #9)

Ki-kinaskin: you're lying

Kisahkahehtin Mistahey: I miss you very much

Kookum: (or *kookoom*) your grandmother (*Nookom*: my grandmother)

Mahkah geegeesh: big baby

Meegwetch: thanks (*Kitchi Meegwetch*: great thanks)

Mistahey: very much

Moonah: no

Moonaneh, gawenah mateh: don't worry, don't cry

Mooshoom: grandfather

Mushkegowuk: tribe named for muskeg (or, *Omushkegowuk*)

Nimama: my mother

Nimeem: my younger sister

Nimis: my older sister

Nipapa: my father

Nisom: my granddaughter

Nitao: hunting, fishing, and trapping in the bush

Nishnawbe Aski Nation: 'the people of the land'

Okimaw: a leader or teacher (teacher is also *okiskinwahamakew*)

Powwow: From the Algonkian word *pau wau* meaning "spiritual leader." It refers to a gathering of North America's Native people that includes singing, dancing, and socializing. The Powwow event is also a way to remember heritage, culture, and traditions among Aboriginal Peoples.

Tipi: (or *teepee*) a cone-shaped, portable wooden-frame dwelling traditionally covered with hide

Wacheyeh: hello (also *wachay*)

Wawahtay Eskwoh: Northern Lights Woman

Wemistukuushuu: white people

Acknowledgments

I learned about Shannen Koostachin while collecting stories about young rights activists, mainly from poor developing countries. When I read Shannen's Peace Prize nomination, I was shocked that such injustice was happening in my own country. The determination of the children of Attawapiskat convinced me to help raise awareness by telling this story.

The loss of any child is an unbearable tragedy, especially in a small, tightly knit community. Shannen was the fifth young person in Attawapiskat to pass away in one year. I'm deeply grateful to her family and friends who spoke with me during their most painful period of grief. I could not have written this book without Serena Koostachin, who generously gave me insight into the life of her sister and closest friend. Thank you, Andrew and Jenny, for your trust. I admire your strength for wanting your daughter Shannen to be an Okimaw to others.

In my fictionalized version of this story, many important people in Shannen's life appear as minor characters. In real life, they are very important, especially Julius, Raven, Mickiso, Codee, Dallas, John B., and Celine Nakogee. Jaban, Theresa Koostachin, entered the spirit world during the writing of this book. May she, Shannen, and Rosa rest in peace.

I was not able to mention every grade eight student in the story, but I appreciate your permission to include photos. Thanks to all who gave interviews, especially Chris, Chelsea, Jonah, Katrina, Ashley, Stephanie, Melany, Mallory, Ocean, Keisha, and to all my new Facebook friends. Thanks to the Attawapiskat parents, especially Evelyn and Raphael Kioke. The residents I met were kind and helpful, especially Rosie Koostachin, John B. Nakogee, Annabella Iahtail, and Joseph Kataquapit—I recommend his inn.

Thanks to everyone who contributed information and photographs. Carinna Pellett, Charlie Angus, and Cindy Blackstock deserve a special mention, as do their assistants, Janet Doherty and Tammy Morgan. They are tireless and devoted advocates for First Nations communities. Go to www.shannensdream.ca to learn more about this campaign.

I appreciate the kindness of my friends who read drafts, especially Jenny Kitson and Clare Henderson. Thanks to everyone at Second Story. Margie Wolfe and Carolyn Jackson understood the timeliness and importance of this story. I appreciate their faith and encouragement. I was blessed with a marvelous editor,

Yasemin Ucar, who was patient, always helpful and hard-working, with a sharp eye for detail. The unflappable Melissa Kaita did a terrific job working with so many digital photographs to make them work on the printed page. I am grateful to the Writers' Union's Writers-in-the-Schools Northern Ontario Program, the Ontario Arts Council, and the Canada Council for financial support. My husband, Chris Wilson, helped at every step along the journey. Thank you for your love and support.

Dedicated to the memory of Brendon Kioke, Dakota Nakogee, Dwayne Hookimaw, Ian Kamalatisit, and Shannen Koostachin.

In Ottawa: Left to right: Norbert Paulmartin, Nelleon Scott, Mike Kataquapit, Marvin Kioke, Joe Paulmartin (behind), Prinz Sutherland, Tara Stephen, Julie Shisheesh, Darren Taylor, Solomon Rae (front), Stephanie Paulmartin, Chris Kataquapit, Shannen Koostachin, Janet Kioke (behind), Jonah Sutherland, Kayla Louttit, Ashley Sutherland, Brendon Kioke (behind), Michelle Kioke, Irene Kioke, Lance Gull, Jenny Nakogee, Emma Wesley, Not shown: Agnes Wheesk

Grade eights who did not go to Ottawa: Gary Shisheesh, Gregory Wheesk, Roman Kataquapit, Isaac Edwards

Photo Credits

Cover (Shannen), Page 92: Charles Dobie; Janelle Wheesk: William Blake; Carinna Pellett and Dean Esligar; Assembly of First Nations

Title page: William Blake; Author's Note: map © Norman Einstein; Aerial photo, Page 6 above: Rod Peters; below: Brenda Stewart; Pages 10, 51: courtesy of Ashley Sutherland; Page 12: courtesy of Carinna Pellett; Page 13: photographer unknown; Pages 18, 26, 78, 154, 177, 180: courtesy of the Koostachin family; Page 21: courtesy of Laurette Edwards; Pages 33, 39: Ronda Potts; Page 24: © *Wawatay News*; Pages 36, 51, 58, 66, 68, 93: courtesy of the office of Charlie Angus; Pages 44, 48: courtesy of Assembly of First Nations; Pages 55, 120, 149: © *Toronto Star*; Page 59: Clinton Hill; Page 67: Terry Chakasim, Page 81, 194: photographers unknown; Pages 87, 88, 94, 98, 101, 112, 114, 162, 203: Carinna Pellett and Dean Esligar; Page 99: © *The Ottawa Citizen*; Pages 103, 182: Chris Wilson; Page

121: Mildred Young Hubbard, Archives of Ontario; Page 133: Cindy Blackstock; Pages 134, 183: courtesy of Chelsea Edwards; Pages 145, 196: Jane Oliver; Page 148: Janet Doherty; Pages 157, 136: Beverly Nakogee; Pages 168, 173: posters courtesy of Wendy Anes Hirschegger, OSSTF; Page 184: Stephen Mau; Page 187: Archives Deschâtelets; Page 195: David Wesley; Page 207: Isabel (Izzy) Tabobandung courtesy Jasmine Koostachin

Every effort was made to identify the photographer of each photograph. Please contact the publisher if you know the name of an unidentified photo.

About the Author

JANET WILSON, an award-winning author and artist, is continually inspired by courageous young people working to make a difference. Her book *Our Earth: How Kids are Saving the Planet* was a Smithsonian Notable Book and winner of the Science in Society Book Award. She lives in Eden Mills, Ontario.